Praise for this Book

Reader in London, England:

As a single woman I try to be careful and smart about my whereabouts and getting to and from them but sometimes that is not enough.... I read Mr. Gordons book and thought how easy the pictures made it look. Then I thought well they were trained professionals doing the moves. Well, I tried one of the moves, and just like the book said, my friend crumpled to his knees. I could hardly believe how fast it worked. It took so little energy. I tried a few more moves, and they also worked. So now I am doing what the author suggested. I'm learning one move a week. Do yourself a favor. Read this book. You need to know how to protect yourself because one never knows when danger will arrive. These simple moves can be the difference for your survival. This book gives you the chance.

Reader in Ontario, Canada:

I highly recommend this book! ... [It] clearly lays out effective defense moves using many photos and clear descriptions, to give anyone a basic knowledge of how to protect oneself from attacks, how to temporarily disable an attacker so you can run away, and tips for avoiding and de-escalating potential attacks. As he [the author] points out, you don't have to be strong or assertive, if you learn what he teaches you can use skill and smarts that can make you more powerful than someone stronger. ...Every woman would do well to read and practice the instructions in this book so that you are prepared and feel more confident living in the world.

Reader in USA:

Clinical Child & Adolescent Psychologist. Ph.D.,

Escape Being Raped or Attacked, Second Edition, is a must read book for everyone who cares about the safety and well being of women. As the mother of three teenage daughters (one of whom will be heading off to college in the fall), I plan to teach these self defense moves to each of my daughters. This book is easy to read, and very effective at teaching important self defense moves. I feel much better knowing that my daughters and I can defend ourselves if we are ever attacked or assaulted. Please read this book, and share it with all the important women in your lives.

Escape Being Raped or Attacked

Using Common Sense, Karate, and Ju-Jitsu

Third Edition, Revised

Ted H. Gordon, J.D., M.B.A.

Third Degree Black Belt, Ju-Jitsu

Brown Belt, Karate

Exclusive Distributors: Amazon.com

Printing: (August. 2022)

ISBN-**13: 978-1727557329**
ISBN-10: **1727557328**

Printed in the United States

Other Books by Ted H. Gordon

California Real Estate Law: Text and Cases

Legal Terminology and Usage: For Court
Reporters and Paralegals

Defend Yourself with Ju-Jitsu or Karate
and Stay Out of Jail

Burdens of the Heart: Surviving Heart Transplant
and Finding Secrets of the Medical Profession

Live. Don't Let Cancer Become Your Life

Summary of Parliamentary Procedure

Individuals with Disabilities Education Act:
Handbook for Special Education Teachers and Parents

Real Estate Principles in California
(Co-Author)

Can Self-Defense

C. Diff. What Is It. How Do You Get Rid of This Disease

Publish Your Book: Turn Manuscripts
into Salable Books

How a Poor Student Became the World's Smartest Man:
The Story of Albert Einstein (Children's Book)

To Madison

May you always have the tools to protect yourself.

With special thanks to

Angie and Peter, Lauren and Andrew, and to the others who so graciously volunteering to pose for the many photographs in this book, including to Veronica, Jill, and Brandy.

Table of Contents

Part V: Serious Attacks

Part VI: Fighting from the Ground

Part VII: Other Attacks

Part VIII: High-Risk Occupations

Disclaimer, Waiver, and Release

Being attacked is a dangerous situation, and no book, including this book, can assure you that the self-defense techniques will protect you, prevent you from injuries, or even be effective in an attack. All the author can say is that in his experience, in a supervised ju-jitsu class with proper training, almost all the students mastering the techniques from this book, have been able to use them effectively in class most of the time. That does not guarantee they will work for YOU.

Your attacker may have special skill you did not realize; the aggressor may luckily move in a way to block a technique; you may be so frozen with fear you will forget or do the technique wrong; you could be so hyped up with adrenaline that you do the move incorrectly or ineffectively; or a hundred other things could render the techniques ineffective. There is no guaranty or warranty that you will be able to make these techniques work during an attack, or that if you do, that you will avoid injury or worse. To the full extent permitted by law, the author makes no warranties, express or implied (including but not limited to implied warranties of merchantability and fitness for a particular purpose). Use the techniques and information in this book at your own risk. THIS BOOK IS PRESENTED SOELY FOR ACADEMIC STUDY.

Neither the author or publisher is liable for any damages, incurred or alleged to have incurred, of any kind arising from the use or non-use of the information or techniques in this book, including but not limited to direct, indirect, incidental, punitive, or consequential damages. You further agree not to sue the author or publisher and to hold them harmless from any all claims arising out of the information and techniques contained in this book. You agree to be bound by the aforementioned disclaimers, covenant not to sue, the release. If you disagree with any of the above, within 30 days after purchase, return this book for a refund and do not use any the information and techniques in this book.

If done correctly the techniques and information in this book can be harmful to the recipient, including severe injury, paralyses or even death. Also, use extreme care when practicing these moves so as not to injure your helper.

As to any lability that could arising from practicing or from using, or attempting to use, these techniques in an attack, check with a local attorney in your state. The line between self-defense and attack can sometimes become difficult to access, and using the techniques in this book might have unintended legal consequences. The author is writing as a layman, with no special legal knowledge.

Further the author is not a doctor and has no special medical training. Any information about what the damage a technique can be done with these techniques is merely based on information provided to the author by his ju-jitsu and karate instructors, and not from any doctors. For reliable medical information, contact a physician.

If any of the above provisions, clause, or word(s), are ruled invalid or struck from the above, all other provisions shall remain in full force and effect.

How to Practice

Be Kind to Yourself. Assume you were standing in the class as I taught, and your neighbor complained of being frustrated because she was not learning the techniques as fast as she wanted. You would most likely look at her and remind the woman that this was a sport like golf, tennis, or skiing, and you do not learn a sport in an hour. It takes time and many repetitions. Be as kind to yourself as you would be to a stranger next to you. It is a sport, and any sport takes time and numerous repetitions. Give yourself time to learn and do not expect to pick up everything on the first attempt.

Dangerous—Practice with Instructor. The techniques discussed in this book can be dangerous, causing severe injury, and presumably even death. They can be hazardous to practice and are even more deadly if done wrong. Make the moves with the help of a qualified instructor who can control the speed and method of performing the techniques and correct incorrect applications. My descriptions of the effects of techniques are a layman's estimate of the damage and not the result of medical knowledge.

Doctors Approval. The practice of the techniques in the book are a form of exercise, and one should never engage in physical activity without a doctor's approval.

Look Out for Your Partner. If you choose to practice without a qualified instructor, never a good idea, remember neither you nor your practicing partner is likely skilled in the martial arts. Take special precautions to protect your partner. Do not ever try to surprise your partner during practice. You are both learning and are not accomplished practitioners.

Similarly, never hit your partner; always stop your punches and kicks several inches from your opponent. Stop immediately if your partner yells "stop" or otherwise suggests submission. In Judo, a double tap on the mat, to yourself, or to the partner indicates surrender and stop all action. Never actually throw anyone to the ground unless both you and your partner know how to fall and you are on safety mats. Be kind to both of you.

Part One

Introduction and Basic Escapes

Chapter 1

Overview

According to statistics, as a woman, you have a 20% chance of being attacked or raped in your lifetime. It is a sad statement about our society that books like this are even needed. Unfortunately, at such a high-risk, you cannot afford to move through life blindly and hope your luck holds out. It requires knowledge and skill to avoid those high-risk situations, and defuse the potential for attack. In those rare cases of actual assault, you must know how to subdue the attacker physically.

Why do so many women freeze when attacked? It is the same reason a soldier often freezes in his first battle. When a new soldier sees bullets flying and realizes the actual danger he is in, the soldier often forgets everything. However, during this freeze, like a zombie, he follows his training. The soldier will load a magazine in the rifle and fire, repeat, and keep often repeating without remembering why he is doing so.

However, when a woman is attacked, and she freezes, if she has not taken self-defense training, there is nothing to fall back on. The woman must fight as best she can, or the woman lady may be forced to stand there like a deer in the headlights and just hope she is not permanently hurt. These techniques give you a well of resources to use against your attacker. Your ultimate goal is _not_ to win the fight, but to _disorient or distract_ your opponent enough so you can escape.

In today's society, no book, no class, no training, can guarantee you will not be attacked. Unless you never leave your house, you are going to be among strangers and in situations where any of those people could theoretically attack you. Actually, as one rape counselor reminded me, even in your own home, you cannot guarantee that you are immune from an attempted rape.

In today's world, you as a woman should know how to protect yourself from rape and other attacks. In the 1950's when I was a child, the front door of our house was always unlocked. In Northern California at elementary schools, we had earthquake drills and nuclear bomb practices under our desks, but nobody worried about children being hurt by adults or about women being attacked while walking in public. Yesterday is history. Today and in today's environment, it is prudent, and unfortunately even necessary, to know how to defend yourselves.

Statistics

The statistics vary, from city to city and by how you define attack and rape. The police department and FBI statistics do not always agree on exact numbers. But, numbers do not always tell the whole story, anyway. If the weather person says there is a ten percent chance of rain today, and you step outside and find it raining, as far as your concerned, there is a 100% chance of rain.

- _Statistically, of every six women in the U.S., one of them has been or will face an attempted rape in her lifetime._ That is a very high statistic and one which should not be ignored! That statistic does not include ordinary non-sexual attacks against you. Add the rape and at-tempted rapes to other attacks and you face a significantly higher chance of being forced to defend yourself. Further, women in specific locations in some cities or in colleges face far higher risks than average.

- *Another chilling statistic is that nationally in 50% of all rapes, the woman knew the attacker.* Sure, you do have cases where the stranger in the ski mask jumps out of the bushes, but in half of all rapes, you know the person. Most violations are committed by friends, family, and past or current dates. You cannot relax your diligence.

- *Over half of all rapes occur at or near the victim's home.* Again, some 15% occur in open spaces like a park, and 10% occur in closed areas like the garage, but the vast majority occur near your home.

- *Only 13% of all rapes were done by an armed attacker.* In 87% of the crimes, the victim is unarmed.

- *20-25% change of rape or attack.* If you add assault and battery to the rape statistics, then during your lifetime you have a 20%-25% chance of being raped or attacked, depending on whether you use police and FBI statistics or the CDC's figures.

Somewhat surprising, at least to me, is the fact that as to just rape, the clothes do not seem to matter. Wear something sexy or wear old clothes that cover you from head-to-toe, and statistically, it does not seem to matter. It is inattentiveness and looking meek that basically makes you a target.

Goals of this Book

This book has two aims. The first goal is to make you realize the risk you face and encourage you to take steps to minimize the chance that you will be attacked. If you avoid high-risk situations, you lessen your chance of being chosen for an attack or an attempted rape.

In other words, what training will do is make you a less appealing target to a would be attacked, because you look prepared and because you keep yourself in safer locations and minimize predicaments.

The second goal of this publication is to suggest techniques to use if attacked. If you are attacked, training should help you defeat the attacker and hopefully allow you to escape.

Why You Can Protect Yourself

Ah, but you say: "Wait a minute. I am out of shape, somewhat shy, not overly athletic, and never been in a fight. I am not a fighter, and I do not know how to fight. What makes you so sure I can defend myself." My answer is easy. I am teaching women in 2018 in Scottsdale, Arizona at age 72, so I know it is skill and technique, not speed and strength, that makes my moves work. But, there is more. Three years ago, I underwent a heart transplant.

So here I am a 72-year old man with an older body, teaching self-defense which I know works because I can do it. Every woman, unfortunately, is probably in better health and physical fitness than me. Yes, I know you can defend yourself in learning these moves and commit them to memory.

Your Role Is Easier Than You Think

What does an attacker have when he jumps out to attack a woman? Indeed, he has the element of surprise going for him. Suddenly and without warning, he has jumped out from a bush or behind an alleyway or door. Supposedly, he has his strength and larger size going for him. Men attack women smaller and weaker than they are. And, most importantly, many Americans are taught to be considerate, kind and unaggressive. And, women are taught further to be gentle.

Actually, when you balance the scale, you find a prepared woman being attacked has a lot going on for her. First, she knows ju-jitsu defense (or else why are you reading this book?). You have the element of surprise because he does not expect you to fight back or even know who to fight. Secondly, while it is usually preferable to counter-attack the minute he attacks, you can theoretically pick your time to strike. You can always play act, yelling "please do not hurt me, I will do anything you want," while you wait for the right time to attack. And, finally, you do not need to win.

Let me re-empathize that last statement. You are not fighting to beat your attacker to a pulp, you are merely struggling to temporarily distract or disable him enough to allow you to run to safety. There is no reason to continue fighting and prove yourself a better fighter (mainly because you might not be); instead, you just want to over-come him just enough to escape. Nothing more.

Rape Trauma

In 2015, a Stanford University swimming student named Brock Turner raped an unconscious woman behind a dumpster. The woman wrote a letter which went viral on the Internet, explaining some of the trauma she suffered. In her statement, the woman wrote:

> *"My independence, natural joy, gentleness, and steady life I had been enjoying became distorted beyond recognition. I became closed off, angry, self-depreciating, tired, irritable, and empty."*

Rape is serious with deep emotional damage. The techniques dis-cussed in this book are essential steps in fighting off an attacker.

Although this is a book about avoiding rape and other attacks, it would be remiss not to at least mention that if you are attacked or raped, you should use the many fine organizations that exist. Since the 1970s and 1980s rape counseling and other physical attack treatments have become accepted, well organized, and very useful.

Very few people survive rape or attack without some post-traumatic stress and often more severe lingering psychological difficulties. You owe it to yourself to at least investigate such organizations.

If you are unsure of where to turn, the most prominent organization in the United States in RAINN (Rape, Abuse & Incest National Network). Besides its own resources, it also created and operated National Sexual Assault Hotline (800.656.HOPE, online.rainn.org and also rainn.org/es). RAINN maintain the hotlines in partnerships with over a thousand local facilities in the U.S. and on military bases.

Chapter 2

Escapes from Grips

Ju-jitsu is the art of attacking your opponent's weak spots so that a smaller, less muscular person can overcome a larger, more powerful opponent. Later this book discusses how to defend yourself by attacking and even injuring your aggressor, but this chapter shows how easy it is to avoid being caught by wrist grips, lapel grips, and other grips without causing pain.

Reason for Pain-Free Escapes

These releases are designed to disengage and free you from your attacker without damaging or harming him. There are situations where you may wish to avoid injuring or causing pain to your attacker. The three most common reasons are: if you are a nurse and you don't want to hurt a patient if you're a teacher and you don't want to harm a student, or if you are at a party and the man who grabbed you is a jerk, but not dangerous.

In such cases, you can effortlessly and calmly break free, and stand back a few steps from the surprised attacker. Then following with a loud verbal command (such as "stop" or "leave me alone" or "if I have to call someone you are going to have serious consequences").

The art of self-defense doesn't mean you immediately have to begin breaking bones or striking vital points. You need to assess the situation when you are first grabbed. If you have been attacked in a dark alley, you need a robust and, painful retaliation to escape a dangerous situation. But if you are at a formal party harangued by an over-aggressive date or a nurse with a violent patient, pain-free escapes are often the best method. You need an option, which is why you learn both painless escapes and escapes causing pain and sometimes injury.

Bones of the Forearm

You will find wrist escapes are easier to learn if you know three terms: radius bone, ulna bone, and "bone out." The radius and ulna bones are part of the lower arm. The radius is the bone on the same side as your thumb. The ulna is the bone on the opposite side of your arm.

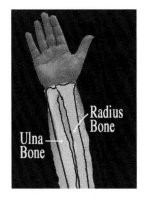

The term "bone out" means to turn your arm so that your ulna or radius bone is facing out. If you look at the front of your wrist (in other words, turn your palm up), you see your flat, wide fleshy wrist. Contrast this front section with the side of your wrist, which is much smaller. More importantly, because it is all bone, that side of your wrist is hard as a rock. Using this part of your wrist to escape is more comfortable and far more effective.

Escape from Wrist Grips

One of the most common ways that an attacker starts an attack against a woman is to reach out and grasp her wrist. The man is generally stronger, and this grip makes him feel in complete control. When a man grips your wrist, his fingers form a vice-like grip. Move against the fingers, and you cannot escape. They will hold you tight. However, the thumb is weak. His hand only has a small muscle controlling the entire lower thumb joint. All of the attacks in this section focus a breaking away by applying pressure against the thumb.

These techniques are surprisingly simple and highly effective, However, if you are having trouble, assume that you are not executing the art correctly. Please re-read the instructions again, especially the section on the "elbow lift."

The first part of the chapter focuses on just the plain escapes, as that is the purpose of this segment. The goal is making you confident that you can escape a man's wrist grip, no matter how firmly he holds on. The end of the chapter adds a punishing counter-attack to the mix, and other chapters show you many more disabling strikes.

Outside Wrist Grip

Your attacker can grab your wrist in many ways. The most common method is the so-called "outside wrist grip." Here, the man reaches out with the hand on the same side of his body as your arm and grabs your arm securely in a strong wrist grip. Since most men are

right-handed, this chapter will assume they reach out with the left hand to catch you. They take a tight grip on your right wrist. If he grabs your other wrist, the book's instructions would be reversed. The escape is a four-step release.

<u>Bone Out</u>. The first thing you do is to make a fist and then rotate your hand about 90 degrees, so your bone is facing his thumb.

<u>Now Augment Your Strength</u>. Step forward with your left foot, while at the same time reach in with your left arm and grab the fist of your right hand. This bar across your secured wrist 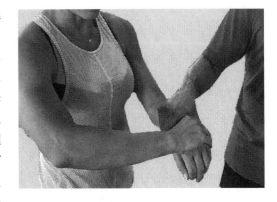 will allow you to engage your entire body in your escape. Instead of just pulling with just one arm, you will now be able to bring your whole body's weight into your getaway.

<u>Elbow Lift</u>. After you gripped your right wrist, bend your elbow, which brings your elbow in towards his stomach. So, this action pries the wrist partly free,  making an opening. By moving your elbow inward, you are using the principle of leverage. Since you are working against the weak side of his wrist, he cannot resist with his strength.

You do not pull your elbow towards you, because he will resist. Instead, as you bend your elbow, you bring your elbow joint close to his hip. As you can see in the above picture, part of your wrist is suddenly partially free.

<u>Body Release.</u> Finally, you step back with your left leg and pull your arm up using your other hand's grip on your captured wrist. You pull up and towards your left ear.

You do not use force, and if you find yourself using strength, you are pulling in the wrong direction. It is the pull of your arms plus the weight of your body as you step back that fully and finally breaks the hold.

Cross Wrist

<u>The Grip.</u> The man reaches out across his body, using with the

hand on the opposite side of his body. He grips your arm. Usually, in this grip, he grabs with his dominant hand, which is his right hand.

<u>Bone-Out Then Elbow-In</u>. Make a fist, then roll your ulna bond towards his thumb. Reach over and grab your fist, and bend your elbow. Be sure to bring your elbow in towards his waist and do not pull back towards you.

<u>Partial Release—One Hand.</u> The picture at right is showing you the move without your other hand like a bar. Many

schools teach this technique without the second hand. I do not favor this method. If your attacker is a powerful man, it will take two arms and your

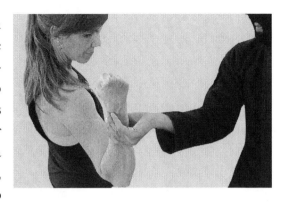

entire body to break the grip. I urge you to practice and always use the two-handed grip. Then you are never unprepared or lacking power.

<u>Final Body Release</u>. Finally, step back with the opposite foot from your captured arm. As before, pull your fist towards your opposite ear.

Two Hands on Forearm

<u>The Attack</u>. The picture shows the attack. He reaches out with both of his arms and grabs your wrist, Both of his knuckles and also the knuckle of your trapped arm are pointed towards the sky.

<u>Bone Out and Augmented Under Grip</u>. Now, roll the bone opposite your thumb (the ulna bone) towards his thumb. Reach under and grab your fist.

Now, step back with the opposite foot as holds your arm. Twist your arm so that the ulna bond facing away from you is snapped back

towards your stomach. It is a little hard to see clearly in the picture, but Angie's knuckles are facing down towards the floor.

Two-on-One Wrist

<u>The Attack</u>. The attacker reaches over and grabs your arm with two hands. One hand has the knuckles facing out one direction, and the other hand has the

knuckles facing out the other direction. His two thumbs are locked, crossed or lying next to each other.

<u>Bone Out</u>. Now, roll the bone next to your thumb (your radius bone) towards your attacker's thumbs. Both thumbs are on top of your arm so your radius bone will be facing up.

<u>Augment.</u> Now reach over and grab your fist. This two-handed grip is a strong one and should only be performed by swinging the augmented arm in coordination with your body movement.

<u>Elbow Life</u>. Pull your elbow in towards his waist. Your arm escapes through the opening between both of his thumbs. Bring your elbow close to his body  and raise it upward in your escape.

<u>Body Release</u>. As before, step back as you pull your arm free. This places the weight and strength of much of your  body in assisting with the escape. Pull your fist towards your opposite ear.

Add Punishing Strikes

The above wrist escape and the other wrist escapes in this chapter are designed to demonstrate that nobody should be able to grab your wrist and retain his hold. The real question then becomes, what is your next step?

The Issue. There are many different strikes you can do from the escape position, but one should be suffi- cient for disorienting him and allowing you to run away.

As you pulled away, your hand is up somewhat near your ear, your feet are apart with your strong side facing his weak front side, and your hips are facing at least 90 degrees or more from his weak front. In this picture, it is your right hand that becomes the striking hand.

The Strike. Flatten your upper hand near your ear so it can be swung is a circular motion towards the side of his

neck. You are aiming for the carotid artery. A strike to this artery should temporar- ily disorient him, may drop him to the ground, and could conceivably even break his neck (although the latter is unlikely).

Now, as you strike towards his neck, be sure to swing your hips and arm in syn- chronization with the swing of your arm. When you hit his neck, the full weight of your body would be behind the strike. Don't just swing your hand, because, without sufficient training, you can't generate enough power to disorient him.

So, as you look at the strike in the picture, notice how your hips which were perpendicular (90-degree angle or greater) are now almost facing your attacker as the blow is delivered.

<u>Backup Second Strike.</u> As soon as your right-hand hits, if he doesn't look or act distracted, follow with your left hand as a strike to his ear. It is not a punch, but a palm strike to his ear. Cup your hand as you slap-strike hard his ear, probably rupturing his eardrum and disorienting him enough to escape.

Lapel Grip

Every grip has its weakness. If a person reaches out and grabs your blouse or coat in a firm grip, to the untrained person, it is hard to disengage. If you push to the right or left you meet their thumb and fist or their fingers curled up in a fist with your clothes. Escaping to the left or right is tough. But the grip lacks strength up and down. Pushing down is the most effective escape, primarily because you can use your body weight and leverage.

<u>The Attack</u>. The attacker reaches out with his right hand and grapes your shit or coat, here as commonly done, just above the breast, in a tight-fisted grip. He could grip anywhere on your blouse, and the escape works from most angles where you can generate room for your ulna bone. This art assumes the situation is such that you do not feel in danger for your health or life and have concluded a pain-free escape is appropriate.

Engage Ulna Bone. Bring your left arm up and over his fist. Your knuckles are facing you, and your radius bone is facing down. It is the bone you are going to apply against his grip. At the same time augment the power of the break by grabbing your left wrist with your right hand. You will now have two hands pushing against his one hand.

Push Straight Down. Now push straight down for six to ten inches with your ulna bone and augmented hand, keeping your ulna bone close against your skin. The key to this escape is keeping your ulna bone next to your skin. Don't push it away from your body. At the same time, step back with your left foot, so his arm is fully extended, and he might even be off balance.

Roll Arm Outward and Step Back, Free. Lastly roll your arm outward, so your radius bone is facing the floor, and is about four or more inches from your body. His hand should be free from your clothes.

Double Lapel Grip

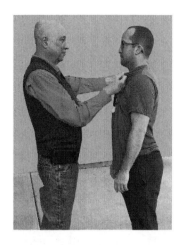

The double lapel grip is considered by some to give one complete control over the victim. Basically, your attacker reaches out with both hands and grabs a secure grip on your clothing with each hand. The assailant now holds your blouse or shit in his right fists. You should automatically take two or three deep breaths to relax before taking action.

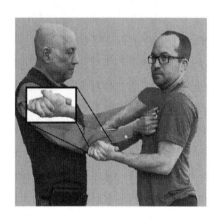

The most important aspect of your first move is that you do not telegraph that you are counter-attacking. Do not move your shoulders. Take your non-dominate hand, usually your left hand, and slide it up and snake it between the attacker's two arms. Grab your other hand in a pancake-like grip.

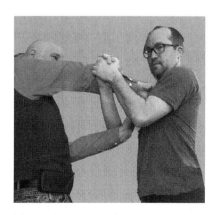

Now rotate your arms upward. Pretend your hands are part of a fixed position gear. You don't move your hands forward or backward. Instead, you raise your hands directly upward, in a circular motion. Note that you do not sacrifice your balance. Your back remains straight.

As you keep moving your hands in a circular motion, your arms will automatically throw off his double grip on your lapel. You are entirely disengaged and separate from your attacker. Since this technique is only a breakaway, no follow-up punishing strike is shown. But, if this were the street, you would use some of the attacks shown later in this book.

Rear Elbow Grip

Attack. The rear elbow grip is a common technique employed by people who feel they have control over you through intimidation because of their position, strength, or verbal threats. While the person can grip you with either hand, most right-handed people will grip your left elbow from behind and begin walking you forward. Surprisingly, most people fail to realize how easy it is to escape from this grip.

Step Forward. Since in this example the person is to your left, you step out with our right foot and plant it on the ground.

<u>Next Step Swing and Pivot</u>. Now when you step forward with your left foot, just swing it around 180° to your right so you will be facing the other way. As you do so twist your arm free. It comes free quickly and easily since the attacker's grip only controls the rear, right and left of your arm. It has no control and very little power preventing you from moving forward. This is why when you step forward and twist, you are free of the grip.

Front Choke

<u>Attack</u>. The front choke happens when someone stands in front of you, usually, with their arms locked straight, place both their hands around your throat. Their two thumbs press into your Adam's Apple or neck, choking you. Such an attack is serious and would not warrant a simple pain-free escape. However, understanding the getaway helps you know how weak an otherwise dangerous grip can be.

<u>Walk Backward</u>. All you really need to do is walk backward, and you can't be choked. Of course, you couldn't do this in the street, because

the attacker would switch to another attack. But try it with a friend. Walking backward does prevent the attacker from putting enough pressure to choke you effectively.

A better pain-free break is to step back with your right foot, but instead of dropping straight back, swing your right foot 90-degrees to your right. Your

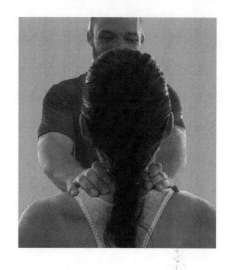

right and left foot should now be parallel to each other, toes facing the same way, and you are effectively 90-degrees to your attacker. (As you will learn in a later chapter, you are putting your body's strong point up against his body's weak point.)

Or, as in the picture, you can step almost all the way around. At the same time as you step back and your left-hand goes up and pushes his hands off your neck. You are now entirely free of the choke. Remember, since a choke is a severe attack, in real life you *not* would risk a simple pain-free escape. Instead, you would follow up with punishing strikes or a violent throw.

Chapter 3

Hair Pull Escapes

Sometimes a man attacking you will grab you by the hair. Since women often have long hair compared to a man, it is easier to grip the hair in a fist and pull. When you are dragged by your hair, your center of balance is thrown off, making it harder to respond. Hair pulling is considered by many untrained fighters as a suitable method of controlling a woman.

Interestingly, when two girls fight, they very commonly grab the other by the hair. It is less so when a man grabs a woman, because statistically they more often do so with a wrist grip, bear hug, or should grip. Still, it happens enough that women need to know how to protect themselves from this type of attack.

I know many instructors that favor arts that pull the little finger back as part of a hair-defense technique. I tend to discourage such moves because when the adrenalin hormone floods your body as part of the "fight-flight response," the ability to accomplish *fine-motor* activities is impaired. It is harder to pull a little finger from a clenched fist holding your hair, while off-balance, and in fear. It is better to concentrate on *gross motor* techniques, like karate strikes.

I've been asked if having long hair makes you more susceptible to being attacked. Statistically, long or short hair makes do difference.

It is other factors like being inattentive to your surroundings, being in dangerous places, not paying attention to others, and the like.

A woman with long hair could be grabbed by the hair in one of Two ways. She could be gabbed in the front of her hair and pulled forward. Alternatively, someone could secure a handful of hair from your rear. You need to know releases from each of these grabs. In both cases when you step, you step low to keep your balance, while blocking the hand holding your hair to loosen the grip, or at least stop being pulled off balance.

Front Hair Grip

The Attack

Your attacker grabs a handful of hair from the front of your head. He usually pulls your head forward to unbalance you slightly and intimidate you. Infrequently he pulls your hair strongly ahead to pull you off balance.

Step Forward

The first thing you do is to step towards him with a big step, sinking into a secure stance, so you are hard to pull forward. Now your strong point, the line between your ankles, is forward towards him. Since he is pulling you ahead, he naturally expects you to resist. But, in true judo principle, you

never resist. He pulls forward, you step forward, only closer and deeper than he expects. Note how strong your balance is and straight your back is in this deep forward stance.

Rising Block

As you step forward, you also simultaneously, strike his arm gripping your hair in an upward motion. Since he is holding your strands in his fist and as your hair is thin and slippery, about half the time this upwards block will completely free your hair. Even if it doesn't, the power of the block will momentarily stun him and stop further pulling since your counter attack is next.

Strike Adams Apple or Groin.

The instant you finish your block, you immediately strike from your strong forward stance. If the throat is open and close, hit the Adam's apple with your fore-knuckles. Or, as here, use the heal of your hand to strike upwards under his chin. As the earlier chapter on "How to Punch" stated, you don't want to punch to the chin as you can injure your hand.

Second Strike

Now strike again, by bringing your other hand forward in a strong, straight punch to the groin. As you do so, remember to look at your

target, and also to keep your fist parallel to your wrist so it is strong and will not bend on impact. He should be disabled enough for you safely escape.

Rear Hair Grip

The Attack

Your attacker grabs a handful of hair from behind you. He will usually pull you slightly backward, or tilt your head back, making it more difficult to stand erect.

Step Backwards and Hands Up

In the next step, you are going to be turning to face him. Since you can't know if he is or will be punching you as you turn, you bring your other hand up by your face to protect it. Now when you turn, your head will have some protection.

As you raise your hands, step to your rear, the same direction he is pulling you. This immediately allows you to gain your balance, by taking a significant step in the direction you are being drawn. As you step back with a wide stance, your hips will lower, and there should be much less pull on your hair.

Pivot on Rear Foot

If you stepped back with your right foot in the previous

paragraph, then you are going to move your right foot. Slide it to your left about two feet from where it was. It should be left of where your left foot is. No Just turn your hips 180

degrees, so you are facing in the other direction. You just rotate on your feet. It would be the reverse if you stepped back 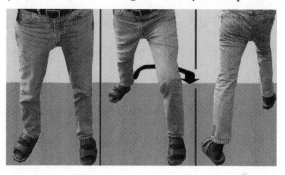 with your right foot. It may seem hard the first time you make this move, but after a few attempts, you will find this is really a very easy stance and rotation to do.

In Japanese Karate, as you take this deep stance, your back leg would be almost straight, and your front leg would be bent. Below the knee, your front leg would be perpendicular (90 degrees) to the ground. Equally important, you back is straight, fully upright, and not bent.

If the Japanese stances complicated, use a position you are comfortable with, as long as your back is straight and your knees are deeply bent and strong.

Rising Block as You Pivot

As you pivot, bring your arm up striking (or blocking) his extended arm that holds your hair. It might dislodge your hair, but the real purpose is to stop or reduce the pulling of your hair.

Strike to Adams Apple

If the throat is open strike the Adam's apple with your fore-knuckles.

If it is not open, change your strike, and use the heal of your hand, strike his chin upward. You don't want to punch him directly in the chin as you can break your hand. See the section "Don't Aim for the Chin" in the chapter entitled "Punching" for details on why you want to avoid punching the chin.

Knee to Groin

Now strike again, by bringing your rear knee into his groin. Since you will be one foot, it is best to grip his shoulder for additional support, so you have a strong stance to generate the power needed to strike the knee hard into his groin. You can also hold on to his shoulder with your hand for more support. He should be disabled enough for you safely escape.

Chapter 4

Handshake Escapes

Handshakes originated during the middle ages in Europe as a means of showing you were unarmed and not threatening a knife. Later, it became the customary greeting of a civilized man in America, and for many women, especially in the workplace. But there are always those individuals who try to use the handshake as a control technique. They grab far too hard, seeking to make you cry or cringe; or, maybe they refuse to let go keeping you hostage. If you decide it is a severe attack on you, as a woman, you need to escape the attacker quickly. Make no mistake, it can be a serious attack.

Serious Release

The Attack

The man grabs you with an unreleasable grip, refusing to let go. Either he wants to embarrass you, punish you, to show his power, or to try to control you. Besides being locked in a grip, it can also be painful. If you deem the hold a dangerous attack, you

need to counter-attack in a meaningful way. For this chapter, assume the attack is considered serious, and you feel you have to react.

Strike the Ribs and Groin

Turn your body sideways and step in towards him. Note you take a deep, strong stance as you slide in close to him. Now cock your left hand by your right ear, then swing your elbow, slamming it into his upper ribs, just below the armpit. Note the shift in weight on the stance and the swing to generate a powerful elbow strike.

(Next, like you are swinging a hammer, rotate your arm at your elbow and bring it back to your right ear. Like a gun that you have to cock before each shot, you have to bring your arm back by the ear to "re-cock" the strike. You need space to generate enough striking power to do damage. Now strike to the groin with a "judo chop" (using the bottom edge of your hand).

Strike to Wrist

If he still has a hold on your hand, and only a few men might then strike his wrist in a downward "judo chop" on his wrist. Use the knife edge of your hand. If you don't feel comfortable using a judo chop, then instead drive a downward elbow into his wrist. Either way, he will release the grip and allow you to escape.

Side Kick to Knee

Usually, the attacker is no further threat to you. If however, you did not strike correctly, and he is still holding on, then bring your right leg up and do a sidekick into his knee.

If he does not drop your hand, keep repeating the sidekick until he collapses or releases your hand.

At Parties and Formal Situations

Ask for Release

Your first step is to ask him softly to let go, and if he refused to acknowledge your request, ask loudly and firmly to the group at large, that this man is hurting you and won't let go. Stating your demand in a loud voice will embarrass most men, and they will generally release you. You may need to repeat the order once or twice more, but usually, it will work.

If Necessary Do Inside Twist Throw

If he still hasn't released his grip, it is time to be far more forceful. Assuming you shook with your right hand, reach out with your left hand and grab his right wrist.

Now that you have two hands on his one arm, you have considerable leverage and strength to move his arm. Raise it just enough so you can duck under your hands, but keep it below the top of his head height. If you try to raise his hand too high, he will try to resist and even consider punching you. Duck under the hands.

As you step under his arm, swing your leg around in a half circle, so you have turn facing the other way. As you do so, you are twisting his arm so sharply, he is thrown to the ground. If he is not thrown at the end of your step, pull down to his rear. He is off balance, and the further twisting of his arm will easily throw your attacker.

Preventing Bad Grip

You can lessen the chance a man will getting a crushing grip on your hand by raising your index finger and pointing it outward. Then when you shake hands, place your little finger on his wrist. This puts your wrist in a strong position, making it harder for him to squeeze. It will protect against all but the active, determined attacker. Many politicians use this technique when they see a big man approaching who wants to shake hands.

Part Two

Basics of Ju-Jitsu and Karate

Chapter 5

Five Mandatory Rules

Five fundamental principles apply to all situations involving the martial arts. You need to study, learn, and use all five principles in your practice and in street-fighting. The five rules are discussed below with the reasons why the rules exist.

1. **Always Attack Your Opponent's Weak Points**.

You do not attack where your opponent is strong; instead, you strike at his weak points. For example, take a man standing up and facing you ready to attack. As he stands on two legs, he is strong along the line between his ankles. That is his strong point, and where you do *not* want to attack.

In the picture at right, the woman, Angie, is laughing because when she tried, Angie found it was impossible to move the man when pushing against his strong point. He was easily able to resist any attack, even from a running start. Most men or women, when prepared, cannot be moved along their strong point.

If you take that line between the ankles, you have the opponent's strong points. Forget his feet and which way his feet are facing. You are using the ankles.

However, if you then draw a second line at a 90-degree angle, that is your opponent's weak point. That is where you attack. The body is always weak at the right angle (90° angle) to the strong line. One of the biggest mistakes many beginners make is they get sloppy and forget to attack at the 90° angle. They strike at the 45° angle and wonder why the opponent is so strong.

In the picture at the right, Angie is lightly pushing against her attacker's chest at the weak direction. She is pushing at the ninety-degree angle against her attacker's weak point, and it takes just a little push to throw him backward, and make a step to keep from falling.

If instead of pushing, Angie targets the attackers back

and pulls on the 90- degree angle, she can throw the attack. Angie takes just one figure on the collar and pulls downward at a 45-degree angle. The attacker will be thrown to the floor.

In knife fighting, one of the moves is that the man attacks you with a knife. He thrusts it straight out towards your stomach. In one technique, all you do is step aside quickly, so harmlessly the blade passes where you were just standing. You have to step to his side, and promptly take one more step, so you are at his rear. Now you take both hands and pull at his collar throwing him to the ground rather violently. It is not an elegant, fancy move, but it is a technique that is very effective. It is just a matter of pulling to the attacker's weak point.

Practice visualizing in your mind the line between a person's ankles as he walks. At the same time imagine the 90-degree angle, his weak point. Spend a day watching people walk, and you will learn to recognize their weak point almost automatically. Then it is easy to know where to direct your attacks.

2. **Ready Stance**.

Of everything in the book, this one technique is probably the most important. When my cousin went to the Mid-East for a vacation and asked for just one technique, this ready stance and how to move with it is what I showed her.

How you face an attacker can have a significant effect on the outcome. Unless you have trained under a different system and are competent in its fighting stance, I urge you to use the Japanese "back stance." I find it an excellent defensive fighting stance against a man in the street. For those of you trained in MMA or Brazilian ju-jitsu, **this stance is not designed for "sports fighting" in a ring.** This is strictly for defensive street fighting.

You need to understand three aspects of the stance: how to assume the stance; how to block and strike from this position; and how to maintain your stance in relation to his body.

Assuming the Stance. Your rear leg is bent and at a ninety-degree angle. It takes about 70 percent of your weight. Your other leg is facing forward, also bent at the knee. It carries about 30 percent of the load.

You are facing almost perpendicular to your attacker, at about a 75-degree angle. Your hands are open, fingers extended and relaxed. Your hand is not in a fist. One of the many advantages of this stance is that you do not look like you are in a fighting position. You look relaxed. *It doesn't escalate the situation by taking this stance.*

To the attacker, you are showing only *your side* and head, but very little of your full body. There is a relatively small portion of your body susceptible to being struck. All your vital organs are out of normal striking range. Compare this stance to standing facing your opponent where  all of your body is exposed. You offer a far more difficult target to hit, which can deter some men just from your stance.

The hand that is on the same side as your lead foot is at a 60-degree angle, with the tip of your top finger about nose or chin high. Your other hand is about three inches above your waist, and parallel to the ground.

Upper Hand Can Block a Punch. If the attacker throws a punch at you, say at your head, all you need to do is move your upper arm about six to 12 inches to block that punch. You make a fist and turn your wrist 90-degrees. Now, your radius bone (thumb side of your arm) and ulna bone (little finger side of arm) are the edges to block. After you move your arm the short distance to block the punch, it returns  back to its original ready position. That hand can move in all directions to stop a blow to the midsection.

Lower Hand Can Block a Kick. If the attacker kicks

you in the midsection or groin area, your lower hand sweeps in a circular motion from the elbow joint. You generally block the kick in a circular motion so you can move the kick aside. You can, but do not usually meet the kick directly as a strike because of the power generated by a kick.

Upper Hand Strike. There are many ways to strike your opponent after you block a punch, but the easiest is to just extend your fist downward from your elbow. This is not a lazy extension of the arm, but a quick snap strike with power behind the backhand action of the arm.

You hit the attacker on his nose with the back of your knuckles. This rear knuckle strike is tough for the attacker to block. Very few fighters are prepared to stop a downward strike coming from a high angle. Usually, all it takes is one or two strikes to the nose to make the attacker realize it is not worth fighting you.

Requirement for Effectiveness

This strong pre-attach position works because two factors are present: both maintaining the proper stance and keeping your strong point to his weak point. You always want to be facing the weak point in at attacker's stance. Since the line between his angles is his strong position, you don't want to be facing his strong point.

Instead, you want to be facing 90° to his strong point—that is, his weak spot is peduncular to his strong point as the chapter already discussed. So, you want to be facing his weak point.

This means if he moves, you must move to keep your strong point facing his weak point. As he walks around, you don't move towards him (an aggressive move) or back away from him (a defensive move). You just keep moving around the circle. In other words, if he takes two steps to the left, you move to the left to keep your angle. You keep moving and shifting directions as he walks, so you maintain your strong stance to weak point advantage.

In the picture, below, Ted's lead foot is forward and on spot "A." As Ted moves, his back foot moves right or left to keep the proper angle to the attacker, but his front foot stays locked in place.

This foot remains on the same spot, just the toes move and pivot around the center point.

The backfoot moves around the circle.

It takes practice to become comfortable moving slowly or quickly, as he jumps around. While doing so, you don't smile, and you utilize your proper breathing techniques. Practice until it becomes second nature. This is one of the most valuable and versatile moves you will probably use.

Breathing. In this stance you begin breathing slow and rhythmically, in and out is a slow pace, countering the effect of the adrenalin bath flooding your system.

Surprise Attack. Of course, some attackers hide in bushes and jump out and grab you before you are even aware they are there. As to them, there is no discussion, and your first move is destroying their attack and escaping. There is no discussion and no time to assume a "ready position." That is another reason why is so important to learn certain defensive moves from the attacker already holding you. However, remember, in 50% of the situations, statistics say you know the attacker, and you have a chance to drop into your "ready stance."

Importance of This Stance. It makes you hard to hit; it is easy to strike full on; and equally important, it does not look like a fighting stance. It should help defuse the situation while encouraging you to breathe properly. It also confuses about one-third to one-half of the potential attackers.

3. **Destroy Opponent's Balance**

Everyone has a center of balance, a point on their body that is in effect the midpoint of where the body is balanced.

Consider a teeter-totter (also called a seesaw) which is a long flat board balanced on a single center point, usually about half-way between the two ends. The board rocks up and down evenly on the center point between the two ends. No matter how the board is turned or rotated around that pivot point, the object remains in perfect balance.

If you move the board closer to one end, the weight changes, and the "center point" or fulcrum is no longer the center of the board, but a spot nearer to one end. But, there is always a center of balance.

Normal Center of Balance

This center of balance applies to all objects, from boxes to people. When a person stands on two legs, usually his center of balance lies near his belly button.

For an individual, who stands on two legs, it is quite easy to destroy his center of balance. If you pull him forward as he leans forward while not moving his feet, his center of equilibrium moves to his solar plexus, which is now located just over his feet. He is easy to throw to the ground. Further, in this off-balance position, it is hard for your opponent to move without first regaining his center of balance over his feet.

New Center of Balance

4. **Never Resist**

You do not ever want to get into a strength contest with your attacker. Besides the fact that he is probably stronger than you and will win in a pushing match, it goes against a vital principle of judo. Never resist.

Assume you get in a pushing match with a man. Further, suppose he has 100 units of strength, and you only have 25 units of force. If he pushes on your chest while you resist and try to push him back, his extra 75 units of strength will easily overwhelm you every time.

Now assume at the moment he pushes with his massive 100 units of strength, you suddenly step back and out of the way, and pull him with your 25 units of power. You now have 125 units to his 100 units of strength, and you win. He is easily moved. That rule is a principal of judo. Do not resist, if he pushes you then fade back and pull firmly; if he pulls you push in that same direction. Done correctly, you will always have greater units of strength then he will because you are combining your joint amount of power.

Another example is pull-pull. So if you are doing a technique where you must pull the man's wrist to the right side of the body, and he resists by pulling towards his left. Fine, you immediately stop pulling to the right and pull him firmly to the left.

5. **Practice Deep Rhythmic Breathing to Counter the Adrenalin Rush**.

When you are scared your body automatically drops into the so-called "fight-flight" response pattern.

The fight-flight response affects all animals, including mankind, when faced with danger. The body is bathed in hormones, and the body undergoes physiological reactions in preparation to either fight the danger or flee from the threat. Without getting overly technical, the adrenal glands secrete epinephrine, which causes the release of the hormone cortisol, while neurotransmitters release dopamine and serotonin. There are other hormones involved as well in this complex cycle.

As a result of the chemical bath, you immediately become "fight-flight" ready. Your blood pressure increases significantly, and your body releases sugar, so you have a burst of energy. Thinking in minute details is inhibited. Digestion slows down as secondary importance as all energy is transferred to your large voluntary muscles which are necessary to fight or flight from the danger. Your vision changes to the so-called tunnel vision, causing loss of your peripheral vision. Often you begin shaking. There is a reduction in fine motor skills making activities like trying to bend someone's fingers difficult. All power is shifted to gross motor muscles allowing you to punch harder and run faster.

When you are relaxed, and practicing the ju-jitsu moves, you can think calmly and in detail. By analogy, think of yourself walking on a treadmill. But, when you are actually being attacked, you do not always have the luxury of thinking clearly. As your hormones bathe you, by analogy it is like running full speed on a treadmill.

I remember an incident that happened many years ago in San Francisco. A student of mine, who had been with the school about two years, was attacked on the street near her home. We always taught moves in a sequence of three different strikes, so in case the first strike did not disable the attacker, you automatically moved on to your second move without having to think what to do next.

The girl later told me with some obvious embarrassment, that she did the first move and the assailant dropped to the ground in pain. However, she was so high on adrenalin, that the woman yelled to the attacker: "get up, get up, I have two more moves." Then, as the adrenalin bath diminished, the girl reddened and realized how foolish it sounded. When you are high on hormones, you do not always think or act clearly.

This is why you practice these moves over and over, at least a hundred and often three hundred times, so they become embedded in "muscle memory." Your forebrain does not have to think about how to react. Instead, it acts upon a pre-arranged sequence of moves already drilled into memory.

One way to reduce the effect of the fight-flight hormonal bath is to breathe deeply and regularly, and by controlling your breathing, you lessen the impact of the adrenaline and other hormones temporarily controlling your body.

Negotiation Phase vs. Fighting Phase

If you watch a fight, there are generally two phases to that fight. Remember that over half of all attacks are by someone you know. Only a minority of attacks occur from someone jumping out of the bushes and grabbing you.

1. Usually, the first stage of the fight begins with the negotiation phase (also known as the "build-up phase" or "peacock phase"). Here, at least one of the contestants puffs up like a peacock showing his plumes. This is the verbal phase. Usually, one or both sides call each other names or make other derogatory comments and effectively challenge or threaten to fight.

2. The second period is the actual fighting phase. This stage is physical contact. Sometimes, especially when two men are fighting, at the start of the physical phase, there is pushing and other intimidation-type action without doing any real physical damage. Then the actual fight begins, with at least one member attacking with full physical contact and intent to do harm. With men, the battle is predominately striking and kicking, whereas, with a man versus a woman, the man resorts mostly to use grabbing and controlling attacks.

Mixed Martial Arts ("MMA"), dominated by Brazilian Ju-Jitsu taught by the Gracie System, is currently the most popular style currently taught in the US. I have found woman trained in the MMA style who are taking my woman's street fighting class frequently misunderstand the Japanese "Ready Position" taught earlier in this chapter. They seem to have a difficult time distinguishing between the peacock phase and the actual battle. Because of their training, they want to assume their primary fighting position, with clenched fists and a stance somewhat similar to a boxer, balancing on the balls of their feet.

In the actual fight phase, you should use whatever system you are most comfortable with. If you are a trained MMA student, then use the MMA stance and fighting techniques if you want. If you have no prior training, then continue to use the Japanese ready position. However, for the *negotiating phase* of a fight, an MMA fighter should not (in my opinion) assume an MMA fighting stance. It is like waving a red flag in front of a bull.

In the negotiating phase, you want to convince the potential attacker that you are not a threat to him but neither are you afraid of him, and he would do well to find someone else because you will not be intimidated. You are trying to de-escalate the fight, and statistically, you have over a fifty percent chance of doing so. But if you escalate and directly challenge the man by making a fist and, from his point of view, daring him to strike you, you are increasing the odds of having an actual attack. I urge you to adopt a neutral de-escalating stance during the negotiating phase and then switch to the MMA fighting stance only if and when the fight shifts to actual fighting.

Interestingly, even Renzo Gracie, twice winner and holder of the Brazilian jiu-jitsu national title, in his book *Mastering JuJitsu*, explains the Gracie system teaches his students to assume the "praying stance" (page 215 of his book) during the negotiation phase. As Renzo states: the "chief advantage of this stance is that it is non-threatening and safe…." The bottom line is almost all systems agree that you do not want to appear aggressive during the negotiating (de-escalation) phase at the beginning of a potential attack.

Chapter 6

How to Punch

When I teach the woman's self-defense class, and we come to the segment on how to punch, I know I am going to have two questions from students. Sure enough, in every class I am asked both questions: (1) Why do I have to know how to punch, and (2) if I learned on a different system, do I have to strike the way you are teaching? Actually, they are good questions and deserve answers.

Why Learn to Punch

The first question is why do I have to learn how to punch? Sometimes, the students say, you do not expect me to trade punches with my attacker. The answer is "I do not expect the students to get into a boxing match." But, on infrequent occasions, it may become necessary to throw a punch or two. It is true, none of the self-defense moves I show students for the basic woman's self-defense course involve punching. However, just because you may not intend to use something, does not mean you should not know that technique.

Knowing how to punch makes you a better student. It teaches you how to throw a punch so that it hurts your attacker. It offers you that option in your repertoire of moves. You never know when the opportunity presents itself, and you may feel the need to throw a serious punch to knock him off balance. Equally important, if you know how to punch, you understand what punching is and how it is done. That knowledge makes it easier to learn how to block a blow. You definitely must know how to deflect a punch. True, statistically, most of the time you will be facing more of a wrestler-type move, but occasionally you could be attacked by someone who likes to hit women. It is hard to defend a move you have not fully understood and practiced, so I teach basic punching. Besides, it is not that hard to learn and makes women realize how powerful they really are.

Different Methods of Punching

I grew up in the Japanese Karate system, where you punch with your whole body. Your punches start from the hip and rotate 180 degrees before striking your opponent. The Japanese are not big people; you rarely see someone 240 pounds and six foot six. It is more likely to find the Japanese karate student is 140 to 160 pounds and under five foot eight. Being fast, limber, strong, but not big, the punching style generates the maximum striking power.

Conversely, the Brazilian ju-jitsu and Korean karate punches are often thrown by a larger, heavier individual. They have the body that automatically generates power as a punch is thrown from their more massive frame. Often, their system is geared towards fighting in the "ring" against another martial arts opponent. They throw a punch from their chin to the opponent. It is neither a better or worse system; it is just a different orientation.

The punches from Brazilian and Korean systems are faster than the Japanese system of throwing from the hip. After all, the blow only travels about 60 percent of the distance of a Japanese punch. Therefore, they are harder to block because there is less reaction time to deflect the strike. And, the Brazilian/Korean system throws more punches in the ring, where speed is domination, and the opponent is fully trained in blocking punches.

Conversely, and maybe this is just my opinion, but in the street, you are not throwing as many punches, and equally important, your opponent is most likely not a trained martial artist. He has not trained on how to block punches. The extra split-second it takes to go the greater distance is not going to matter. Further, most women's builds are of smaller stature, and a more powerful punch is to their advantage.

Why Punch Your Method

From a self-defense point of view, it does not matter what system's style of punching you use, as long as you master that punching technique, and practice it sufficiently to burn into your "muscle memory." What is important is that you know a technique to throw a punch correctly and that can punch in an emergency situation when all the adrenaline is flowing, and your body is acting on automatic.

My suggestion is that if you already know a style of punching and the Japanese techniques I am demonstrating does not interfere with your existing system, that you learn my style. Then, when you fully understand and can do my method of striking, you can compare the two systems. Pick whichever one you think is best for you. It is hard to evaluate two different ways if you do not fully understand both styles. So, you learn both methods, to have the option to decide which is the most advantage for you in the street.

How to make a Fist

You do not just clench your hand to make a fist and throw a punch. If the fist is not correctly held, you can break your hand striking a hard object like a bone. While it is not

hard to learn to make a fist correctly, it does take some simple under-standing of the physics involved.

First, curl your fingers tightly into a fist, then fold your thumb under-neath you fist. The thumb should be below your fist and back out the line of fire, so when you strike the opponent your thumb will not touch his flesh. You do not want your thumb to get caught in his clothing or touch any part of his body. But, most importantly, you want your fist to be at a 90-degree angle to the top of your hand. See the picture on the previous page.

This means that if you rest a ruler or small stick on your forearm, your fist is in a direct straight line with your forearm. If your fist is turned up or turned downward, you can break your hand striking a strong

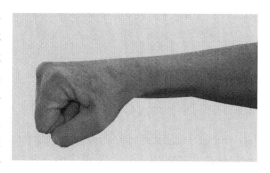

hard surface like the bones in his ribs or the chin of your opponent. A fist that is bent up or down could continue moving upward or downward in striking the object, spraining or even breaking your wrist. Your fist should be a solid extension of your forearm, absorb-ing all the power of hitting an object throughout the entire arm, rather than settling in the wrist.

Finally, you do not hit with all the knuckles of your hand striking the target. Instead, just the first two knuckles next to your thumb strike your opponent. If you look care-fully at your hand, you will note that those knuckles and fingers stand together and slightly ahead of the rest of your knuckles. Just

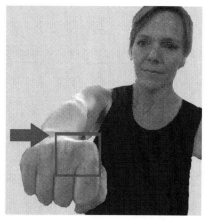

as a thin object has greater penetration power, so do the first two knuckles have greater striking power than your whole fist. You do not want to dissipate your energy too much over a large surface, and your fist is stronger and more powerful using just the small striking area of your two knuckles.

How To Punch

There are many ways of punching in a Karate system, but since you are just learning beginning self-defense and not working towards a belt in Karate, you only need to master the basic punch.

Ready Position

Start with making a fist and putting your hands on your hips. Your fist should lightly touch your hips, with your knuckles down towards the floor. (See the picture at the right.)

Middle of Punch

Thrust your hand forward until your elbow touches your hip. In effect, this part of the punch is like an uppercut, with great power. You should have enough power in your punch to almost crack a floating rib. This is why a woman is able to produce so much power with a punch, unlike the simple power generated from a punch thrown from your chin. As you thrust your fist forward, your

palm remains face-up towards the sky, and your elbow stays next to your hip.

End of the Punch

Turn your hand over quickly and strike your target. Your hand turns 180 degrees so that your knuckles are now facing the sky. The punch should snap out hard and fast. The punch travels in a straight line, and the elbow remains in a straight line and does not flap out away from the body.

Your punch should be aimed at your opponent's solar plexus, the indentation in your rib cage between your breasts. Thus, when you are striking, you are hitting the spot between the middle of *your* body.

In this picture, the punch to both the center of the opponent's body, the solar plexus and is also precisely in the center of Angie's body. Your fist is not off to one side of your body or to the other side. When you are doing repeated series of punches, one fist should quickly replace the exact location just vacated by your other fist.

Mistakes to Avoid

There should be no shoulder push. The punch should fully be extended, but your shoulders should not have moved. You do not push the punch with your shoulders. They are locked in place. Your hand and wrist are locked and

supported by your whole arm, your torso, and your hips and legs. Pushing your shoulder forward is robbing the punch of the power you generated in throwing the punch.

No elevation of shoulder. When you throw the punch, it should come from your arms, and merely pivot through your shoulder. Your shoulder should not raise as you punch. It should be frozen at your side. Sometimes if your shoulder is tense, it can have a tendency to rise.

How to Practice

I have found the best way to practice throwing a punch is to stand facing a mirror, either a full door mirror or maybe a mirror on a chest. Watch yourself and throw the punches soft and comfortable, learning how it feels to throw a punch in a new manner. Once you are comfortable throwing a punch with either hand, start throwing one punch as your other hand withdraws and pull it is fist back to your hip, knuckles down.

Now that you have the motion down and can comfortably throw a slow, lazy punch, while still in front of the mirror, practice throwing the punch at full power, quick and hard. You will note that the faster you withdraw the opposing hand back to your hip, the faster your punch is ultimately thrown. It works like a rotation gear. One arm thrusts out in a punch as the other hand is quickly withdrawn into the ready position next to the hip. Your muscles tighten sharply at the end; if you have your muscles tense the whole way through the punch, you lose power and especially speed.

If you have never punched a heavy bag, then it might be beneficial to strike something offering moderate resistance. This helps you understand the feeling and effect of hitting something solid. It also enables you to keep your wrist straight. There are anatomically correct hard rubber torso and head that you can buy. They are excellent but expensive. A simple method is simply to hit a sofa or mattress on a bed.

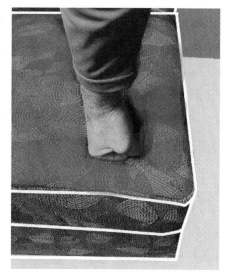

At first, hit softly until you are used to the resistance, before unleashing more powerful and faster strikes. Striking a mattress or sofa is not the same as striking someone, but it is a good practice tool to develop your punching.

Finally, you want to be standing in a comfortable forward stance. In karate classes, you would be a forward stance (called zenkutsu dachi). But, you are not striving for a belt, so select any comfortable stance where your front foot is forward, and your back foot is about three feet apart.

If you are standing with both feet parallel to your shoulders, you are weak. You are punching forward, and an "equal but opposite reaction" and pressure against your punch will be to your rear. Standing parallel your weak point is 90 degrees to the line between your ankles, which is the exact direction of any push back. If you want to do any Internet research, the punch is called a "tsuki" in Japanese, loosely translated as a thrust punch.

Don't Aim for Chin

Do not punch directly to the chin. The head is hard. I heard someone on TV say it wights about the same amount as bowling balls. It might be true. It is a hard bone. As the famous boxer, Mike Tyson found out on August 24, 1988. Tyson got into a street fight and hit the man in the head with his fist. The result for Mike Tyson was a hairline fracture of one of his fingers.

There are better ways of hitting the head instead of a straight punch. Strike it instead with clays at the eyes, a knife hand to the neck, an elbow to the chin, a hook punch, or any other non-straight punch.

Chapter 7

How to Block

A *block* is a method of deflecting a punch by using your arm to move the punch's path. If you analyze a little physics, you realize that all the power of the punch is going forward. It takes only five pounds of pressure or less to deflect the blow by using an arm to move that punch sideways.

Nature of a Block

Japanese karate uses punishing blocks that defend you while often hurting the attacker's arm. These blocks are very effective, but because they are complex, they take considerable skill to learn. Since you are not learning a Karate system, but just a small subset of how to defend yourself against the "general" punch, you will be using simple type block. Its greatest feature is that is easy to learn. The block is effective against roundhouse punches.

The downside is the simple block does not leave you a strong position to counter-attack. Such limitations would matter if you were fighting in a ring or in a boxing type attack. However, you are unlikely to encounter numerous strikes against you in an attempted rape or other offenses.

It is the author's opinion that for your purposes a simple block is sufficient. Statistics show most attacks against woman are grabbing types of attacks and not strikes.

The situation is reversed when two men are fighting. They mostly throw strikes and punches at each other. Understand, if you are really interested in learning a complete self-defense package, you will need to learn more complex blocks.

Roundhouse Punch

The average person in a street-fights throws a strike commonly called a "roundhouse punch." It is called a roundhouse because it does not go directly forward to the target. As you saw in learning how to throw a karate punch, throwing a straight punch is hard and takes training and skill. Few street fighters have the background to throw a straight punch. Instead, they strike with a roundhouse punch.

A roundhouse punch also called a haymaker in some locations, is a punch that is made swinging the arm in an arc instead of a straight jab. This is a more natural punch and one used by untrained fighters. It uses the shoulder as a pivot, and the striking arc means the punch swings wide and rounds in towards your face. It can carry significant power because it comes at a swinging arc, but it easy to block if you know how.

Using the Simple Block

The block is simple. Just make a fist and put it next to your ear, as if you were scratching your ear. The punch will hit your hand by your ear, lose all its

momentum and power, and land harmlessly and painlessly against your arm. It is a simple block because you do not have to track the blow and seek to deflect it. Instead, you let the strike come to you and catch it somewhere on your forearm. In fact, many students have initially said it sounds too simple to work, yet it works well and effectively against roundhouse punches. The block is often used in the ring during professional boxing matches.

Variations of the Block

If your attacker is punching to your mid-section or other parts of your body besides your head, you move your forearm back and forth to block the punch. It takes more coordination for lower blocks since you are  reaching out to the punch. Such is unlike waiting for the blow to come to you. Still, select the block that is most comfortable to you and perfect it.

Others do the same action but use their hands to push to punch aside. If I am not using a classic karate block, I use the surface of my palm (like a "judo  chop") to strike the person's wrist. It is all the same action, just a slightly different part of the body. However, the palm push and the judo chop takes more skill, and practice then does the simple fore-arm block.

In an unusual situation when someone is throwing a straight punch, especially a left jab, it is likely that he has had some boxing or martial arts training. The simple elbow-by-the-ear block will not work against a straight jab. In the unlikely situation, you find yourself faced with that experience, kick and then run fast. He is probably more than an average street brawler. It happens too infrequently to spend time covering techniques like parries that take a fair amount of time to learn to use in combat.

In summary, statistically, men rarely begin punching a woman, as they do when fighting other men. Instead, with women they grab them.

Chapter 8

How to Kick

A kick is an excellent offensive weapon that allows you to strike more powerfully than a punch and with a longer reach than any other weapon of your body. But for a woman learning to defend herself, she only needs to learn one simple kick just to have in her repertoire. You should not ordinarily require a kick in protecting yourself, as your goal is to quickly and temporarily disable your opponent, so you can run to safety. You are not trying to win a fight, you are only seeking to escape.

The average untrained American kick uses the hip as the rotation (pivot point) of the kick. The kick is usually straight legged or relatively straight leg, and swings in an arc towards the target. Often the person licking is unbalanced and the kick while strong, carries nowhere near the potential power of a karate kick.

In karate, kicks can be to the head, shoulders, solar plexus, waist, or any other part of the body. For a woman learning just one straightforward kick, the front kick is a simple forward kick aimed below the waist. Kicks below the opponent's waist are harder to block, require less training, and leave you in a stronger body position than higher kicks. Some schools teach the front kick using the shin bone of the leg as the kicking surface. Japanese karate uses the ball of the foot.

The kick is more focused and allows you to be at a longer distance from the target. There is no such thing as one form is superior to another, it is just a different way of attacking.

Advance kicking methods use side kicks, roundhouse kicks, rear kicks, flying kicks, and many other types of kicks. Since your goal is merely defensive, all you need to know is one kick, the basic front kick.

Karate Front Kick

The karate kick is a four-step movement. You start in a relaxed position, with one foot forward. Shift your weight to the front foot but do not do so in an obvious manner. Otherwise, you will be telegraphing that you are going to kick.

Now, the second step is to thrust your knee up to just below waist height. The movement of driving your knee upward is a strong move generating great power. Think of it as if you were striking someone with your knee. Your lower leg is hanging down towards the ground, with your foot parallel to the ground. It is preferable to curl your toes upward at this stage so you will strike with the ball of your foot and not your toes. You have a little more flexibility if you are wearing shoes as they help protect your toes, depending on the type of shoes you are wearing.

When you kick be sure to lower your center of gravity and bending you non-kicking leg and leaving it firmly on the ground. Do not raise up on your toes when you kick; keep and retain the same low stance.

After the kick, return your foot to the ground as quick as you can, so you are not left standing wobbling on one leg.

Third, you snap your lower leg forward, using your knee as your rotation point. As such, you can not kick any higher than your knee, as the knee is your pivot point. Your lower leg snaps out fast and hard. In doing this action, you roll your hips forward and strike your opponent with the ball of your foot.

The fourth and last step is to swing your lower leg back to the position before the snap. You do not drop your leg to the ground or move the location of your knee. You snap your foot back to the original position, and then, and only then, return the leg to its original resting place on the ground.

The quick, fast snap back to rest foot next to your other knee makes your kick more powerful, renders your leg more challenging to catch or block, and gives you better balance during the kick. The Karate terms for this kick is "Mae Geri" and you can see great pictures of all the steps in the kick by searching the Internet.

Chapter 9

Pressure Points

Pressure points, also called "vital spots" or "tender spots" are places on the body where mild pressure produces a disproportionate amount of pain and discomfort. It some cases, the pressure points can cause loss or an organ or dislocation, and theoretically, even death in some cases.

In Japanese Karate, the discovery is given to an 11th-century warrior. But, vital points (meridians) have long been studied in traditional Chinese medicine and also in Indian medicine. Whatever benefit pressure points may have in medicine, if any, some points when struck produce intense pain and even significant damage.

Someone in the class always seems to ask if there is a *death spot* you can hit to kill the attacker instantly. Theoretically, you could strike the breastbone above the heart so forcefully that it could push the chest bones into the heart, bruising the heart. If you damaged the upper right atrium (sinoatrial node where the electrical impulses of the heart originate), it could cause the heart to go into fibrillation, and you could die in about 60 seconds. But such a strike (probably an elbow or a kick) would need perfectly delivered at an exact location on the chest. In short, possible, but improbable. I suspect a forceful Karate chop to the side or back of the neck could kill someone instantly, although it would more likely injure or paralyze the opponent.

They are many ju-jitsu techniques to choke the person to death, twist and break his neck, and other damaging moves. Clearly, two quick punch or elbow strikes to the kidneys could so damage the kidneys as to lead to death eventually. But, all of these discussions are different from what television shows present as the "instant death" move.

Pressure Point (from the Front)

Remember the song: "eyes and ears. Then down the middle, throat, solar plexus, and groin. Finally, fingers and toes." (Actually, toes mean instep.)

There are many pressure points on the body. There are seven that especially easy to reach, require only moderate striking power, and cause significant pain and damage. Those are the ones this book emphasizes. Too many spots and it is hard to remember in a fight with adrenalin flowing. Learn these, and they should be sufficient for all your needs.

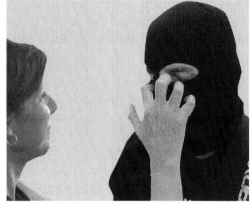

Eyes

The eyes can be struck with a strike by the fingers in the eyeball, itself. Generally, this results in debilitating pain, damage to or loss of eyesight or injure the eye socket and other damages. Because the eyes have sockets or bone behind them, the eyes are generally struck with the fingers bent just a little. The fear is that if the fingers are stiff and straight when they penetrate the eyeball and hit the bone behind, it might injure the fingers.

Of course, you could always just hit the eye with a fist, generally resulting with a black eye and possible damage to the eye socket. However, that takes strength and accuracy, and most importantly, it might not be painful enough to stop the attack on you.

On a personal note, I believe juries react negatively to loss of one's eyesight. Blind people with a white cane slowly meandering up to the witness box disturb jurors. I would only strike to the eyes if the person held a gun or I felt my very life was at stake. Otherwise, I would aim for less damaging pressure points. You will have to decide if you are in such imminent danger to strike the eyes. You also should know the laws of self-defense in your state. It is a very effective strike.

Ears

Here you cup both hands and slap them hard and forcefully against the attacker's ears. The air pushed into the ear canal with the slap can occasionally rupture the eardrum, causing severe pain, loss of hearing, and sometimes leading brain injuries. As in many pressure points, a moderate simultaneous strike to both ears can produce a disproportionate amount of pain and injury.

Throat

The indentation in your throat, just below the Adam's apple, known in anatomy as the supra-sternal notch. This can be struck with a "judo chop" using the base side of the hand, or striking using the fingers was the weapon. Even a mild strike produces a severely debilitating sensation. I guess if you crushed the trachea you could even kill someone. It is an effective but dangerous strike.

Solar Plexus

The solar plexus is about two inches below the sternum, the long flat bone in the center of the check to which most of the ribs connect. The very bottom of the sternum is called the xiphoid process,

and the solar plexus is just below that spot.

A strong punch, kick, or elbow strike to that region can injure organs in the chest, damage nerves below the solar plexus, and cause the diaphragm to spasm making it hard to breathe. Properly delivered the strike will double the person over in pain, making it easy for you to flee the location. An overly powerful strike can compress the chest or rupture the xiphoid process pushing the bone into organs. I was told a strong attack could even kill the person, although I am not sure if that is scientific truth or just a myth.

Be very careful when practicing on a friendly opponent, as this can cause considerable pain and even severe damage.

Groin

A kick, punch, or other strikes to the groin of a man should temporarily disable that person. One of my fellow instructors in San Francisco once had a student who had undergone a sex change operation and looked like an attractive blond woman. I asked her if she  could explain to a woman how it felt for a guy to be kicked in the balls. "Yes," she said, "it is like someone firmly grabbing your nipple in their thumb and forefinger and twisting as hard as they can. Multiply that pain by ten, and you have the effect of kicking a man between the legs."

While I cannot speak to the accuracy of the statement, I can say that if a man is kicked or struck in the groin hard enough, he will immediately collapse on the ground, rolling in pain, for at least five minutes or longer. There is no question a kick or strike, even by a semi-trained woman can devastate a male attacker.

Beside debilitating pain and temporary paralysis, the strong strike could crush the testicles, causing sterility, and possibly injure or rupture the bladder, releasing urine into the abdominal cavity.

Fingers

The fingers are very sensitive and very easy to grab and bend in directions they are not designed to go. Aikido and ju-jitsu make frequent use of fingers to gain the release of holds, to force the person to go where you direct ("comealongs"), and in Karate to break the fingers. The fingers are very tempting targets, but they are seldom just hit with a fist.

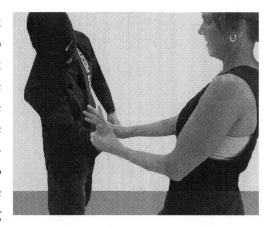

Toes (Instep)

The instep is that portion of the body located between the ankle and the foot. It is on the top of the foot just below the ankle on the mid-line. It is very susceptible to a downward strike with the heal of the foot, especially if you have shoes on. The attack will cause pain, and possibly permanent injury to the foot and the ability

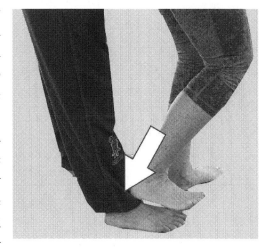

to walk. This is an especially attractive spot when you are grabbed behind in a bear hug.

Pressure Point (from the Back)

For your point of view looking for easy to hit targets, there are fewer from the back than the front. Some people add the rear of the knee to the list, but in my opinion, it takes more skill and understanding to know how the knee correctly. Hence, I suggest all you need is two targets.

Base of Neck

A strike to the base of the neck, hitting about two inches below the bottom of the skull, can cause significant damage. It could knock a person out, break a vertebra paralyzing the person, definitely cause considerable pain and possible confusion, caused a pinched nerve, compress the intervertebral disc space. The strike could cause spasm and whiplash injuries to the brain. It is possible to cause death with a powerful strike delivered to the right area.

This is a very attractive spot to strike from the back when you are in serious risk of harm. Usually, the attack is done with the edge of your hand in a "judo chop" type action.

Kidneys

From the back, the kidneys are a very open target, located just above the belt line in the sides of the back.

Striking a kidney can rupture the organ, damaging a person's health if the other kidney is not sufficiently healthy. It will usually cause immediate pain disabling the attacker.

Chapter 10

Makeshift Weapons

There is nothing that says you cannot be armed with a weapon, even if that object is not a traditional weapon. In feudal Japan and Okinawa farmers were forbidden to have weapons, and so developed a complete system of armed combat with farm utensils. The most famous weapon of all is the six-foot staff or pole. There is a whole system of defense of swinging and thrusting the staff with two hands called bo-jitsu. The smaller versions of the staff are the "club," about two feet long, and favored worldwide by police in the 1800s and 1900s.

Another weapon is nunchakus or chain-wood, and it is still taught today in many martial arts schools. These are the two rounds sticks connected by a small chain and swung with great speed and power and an attacker's weak spots. Of course, anything can be a weapon if it is used correctly, including a fan, a fork, keys, pens, and the like.

I know many books on self-defense for woman hype the benefit of holding your keys in your fist with the key sticking out like knife blades. In my opinion, such an approach looks intimidating but is impractical in practice. First, the keys are on a ring, and putting the ring in your hand and closing your fist around the keys, means if you hit a heavy object, the keys are going to dig into your hand. Try it, use your keys and strike a "heavy bag" at the gym. More importantly, you have the natural weapons of your fingers and fists that deliver more power than with keys. You hold back punching with full force with keys because it hurts.

As with other chapters of this book, there is no attempt to present a comprehensive summary of various items that can be used as weapons. Instead, the aim is to provide you with just enough tools to escape your attacker and flee. It is not to overwhelm you with techniques, each of which, take time to master. You are not leaning a full system.

Magazine

Magazines make an excellent weapon; they look natural, arouse no curiosity, and are effective. The first thing is to roll the magazine up into a tight roll. You want the bound end of the magazine to be the end. The side with the end of the pages should be the center of the rolled-up magazine, where it will not separate in use. Hold the rolled magazine in your hand, with about two to three inches sticking out from the bottom of your hand. You are now able to thrust with the front end, use it like a club, as well as claw with the back end of the magazine.

Let your hand dangle down by your side, holding the rolled-up magazine parallel to the ground. As you approach your attacker, or as your attackers approach you, suddenly raise your upper arm and thrust the newspaper into his neck.

What makes this move so effective is that your shoulder does not move. There is nothing to telegraph the attack. Your arm pivots at the elbow, and only the upper arm swings up to strike your opponent in the throat. The entire rest of your body is frozen and shows no movement. The swing of the upper arm is below his line of sight and therefore is a surprise attack.

You could also make the same attack to the man's groin, but in my opinion, the throat is a better target for temporarily disabling your opponent.

Self-Defense Pen

Several manufacturers sell combat pens over the Internet. These are pens mostly made of aircraft aluminum, which are very strong and surprisingly light. One end is, in fact, a pen which works and you can make notes. The other end varies. The one I like has sharp teeth for gouging the skin, and it also collects skin samples for DNA analysis to catch who attacked you. Just search "combat pens" or "tactical pens," for a list of pens, most cost approximately $18 to $25.

I have never had a problem carrying them on airplanes and getting through TSA security, and I suspect they are probably lawful to carry.

I recommend gripping it about an inch from the end, in what I call the knife grip, with the point towards your thumb. From this position, you can stab the neck or face.

With this grip, you can backhand the rear end across his face like a hammer. Personally, I mostly use the back end like a hammer. The secret is that like hitting a nail, you do not just tap the nail once. Instead, you keep striking until the nail is entirely in. So too, you continue striking, repeatedly, until your opponent withdraws.

Use of Belt

If you have a sturdy, wide belt, with a heavy buckle, it can make a formidable weapon. Grab the end of the belt (the side without the buckle) and wrap it around your hand a turn or two. Then close your thumb and wrap it one more turn around your wrist. Now grab the belt in your hand.

Swing it back and forth in a figure eight, weaving a strong, intimidating barrier in front of you. If your attacker does not back off, he will know the length of your belt and the safe distance to be free of your swing. This is where the extra wrap around your wrist comes in. When you are ready to strike him in the head, you allow the extra wrap around your wrist to come free. All of a sudden, and without warning, your belt is longer and can reach your opponent who mistakenly believes he is out of the danger zone of your belt.

Do Not Use Purse

Students always ask if they can use a purse. I do not encourage the use of a purse. First, it is slower to swing and would probably do much less damage if it hit a part of the body. Someone might be able to catch the purse, and therefore the person wielding the bag. Equally important, if your keys or wallet falls out, you might be tempted to pick them up. If it is your keys, you might not be able to drive away, and your house key might be traceable. If you lose your wallet, besides its loss, you are providing the full address and description of who you are.

Rape Resistant Underpants

Well, I have never seen a pair of "rape resistant underwear," but it sounds encouraging on the Internet website. So, I am suggesting their use without actually seeing the underpants. I am not endorsing any brand because I have never examined any types. One company claims to use cut proof straps in building their underwear that means it cannot be cut with a knife. Further, because a woman's waist is usually smaller than her hips, the underwear cannot be pulled down unless unlocked by twisting the button to a certain angle, much like a dial combination. Since the pants cannot be cut, pulled down, or removed, you cannot be raped. You can decide if it might be worth exploring.

Part Three

Reduce Your Risk

Chapter 11

Reduce the Risks in Your Life

Life is a process of balancing the potential harm versus the inconvenience. How much bother are you willing to accept while opening yourself to the risk of a vicious attack? Obviously, there is no one answer, and many facts influence your decision.

When you are young, many women cannot believe anything will happen, so they discount the risk of any harm. I remember in high school skiing having drunk too much alcohol and worse yet, traversing steep mountains that were really too advanced for me even when sober. I just figured I was indestructible and something would happen to the other guy. It always did, but not because I correctly balanced the odds. I was stupid, and fortunately very lucky. Taking high risks is a risky business. I, thankfully, did not have to suffer the consequences of my dangerous behavior.

Balance Your Risk

To be safer, you have to be willing to accept a little less risk, take a somewhat better protection of yourself, and avoid situations of potential danger. Naturally, you cannot control all threats because beforehand, you do not know what is really dangerous. Instead, it is a matter of acting more prudently, seeking to lower the risk factor.

I agree risk does not necessarily mean danger, but again is the terrible harm (rape, beating or worse) worth the convenience of taking the easy way? If you want to reduce your chance of an attack, you need to reduce the number of situations that carry a higher risk. It is frustrating, hard to do sometimes, and makes you less trusting of society and people in general. You can not live to be afraid of the world. You just want to lower your risk level.

Example of Risk Reduction

Do Not Look Like a Victim

Perhaps, most important, look self-assured and aware of your surroundings. Statistically, most women attacked are looking timid and easily intimidated. Alternatively, they appear so distracted by their cellphone or music devices that they can make themselves an easy target.

Even though I never did criminal law when I was an attorney, attorneys in my office did. Over the years, I talked to many criminals in our waiting room. They all told me basically the same story. The criminals expected eventually to be caught because the longer you engage in criminal activity, the greater the criminal's risk becomes. The criminals all wanted to pick *timid looking women* or *women so distracted* that they would be unaware of their approach. Criminals choose easy "marks."

Grayson Study

There is a significant study done in 1981 by sociologists Grayson and Stein, entitled, "Attracting assault:

Victims nonverbal cues." The study took place in New York, where the sociologist filmed numerous women walking during the day. The videos were shown to rapist and murderers in prison, who were then asked to pick which woman they felt would likely to be attacked.

One unexpected and surprising result was the finding that almost all the inmates shown the pictures picked the exact same woman from the vast array of people like the ones likely to be raped or attacked. The researchers never expected such consistency. The second unexpected result was that all the criminals could tell within seven seconds who they would have picked as a likely victim.

Many signs advertised that advertised a woman would make a good target. The three most significant factors are posture, stride, and gaze.

1.   Posture. Posture is it easy to understand. If a woman is bent, with rounded shoulders, and looking down, she appears as a victim. In other words, for safety you should walk with your back straight can your head up. The old adage a practicing to walk balancing a book on your head is the type of carriage you need.

2.   Stride. The length and speed of a woman's stride was another factor is being a victim. An unusual stride is an indicator of insecurity. The average person walks at a moderately brisk pace, keeping up with any pedestrian traffic nearby. If you walk too slow, or unusually fast, it telegraphs insecurity. Therefore, you want to walk at a regular pace, with a smooth and

ordinary step, arms swinging naturally.

3.   Gaze. The last major indicator is your gaze. Don't walk with a downward gaze, looking at the ground or with a preoccupation with something in your hand. Keep our gaze straight ahead, level with your posture, and briefly scanning the sides and your path. This way you can't be surprised by someone.

Inviting Attack -- Looking Timid and Insecure

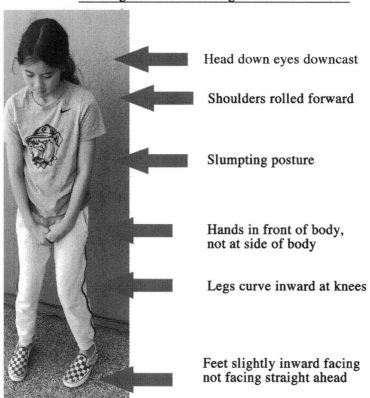

Head down eyes downcast

Shoulders rolled forward

Slumpting posture

Hands in front of body, not at side of body

Legs curve inward at knees

Feet slightly inward facing not facing straight ahead

If you see a stranger approaching, glance at him, holding your gaze for a few seconds, so he knows you've seen him, then move your gaze elsewhere so as not to be challenging that person.

4.   Isolation. There is one other factor, not part of the study, but a vital element in your risk of being attacked. The assailant does not want witnesses, so he looks for isolation. If you walk alone in an alley unseen by others, stride by a grove of trees in a park where anyone can grab and hide you, or meander down a poorly lit street at midnight, your risk fact has risen significantly.

Summary

They were some men who their attack was just a crime of opportunity when they suddenly and unexpectedly found someone in a dark alley or isolated spot. In short, you cannot avoid all risk, but you can reduce your risk. I would guess that you could reduce your risk at least by half, and probably a great deal more, just by striding down the street, back straight, head up, gaze forward and checking your side, while walking in a normal pace, and in a natural manner (arms swinging in a relaxed way).

If they saw a woman, head up high, looking around, walking briskly and purposefully down the street, looking and acting unafraid they left her alone. To them, it was not worth the risk. There were too many other timid or unaware women around who posed a lesser threat.

When you walk down the street, look and act unafraid. As Shakespeare said: "Assume the practice if you have it not, for constant practice can change the stamp of nature." You do not have to be brave and self-assured, you just have to act the part.

In Parking Garage

If you come out of the stores or wherever to get in your car, and you see a car parked next to you with a lone man sitting in the passenger seat, you should go back to the store and have someone walk you to your car. You hear stories of a guy in the passenger seat jumping out as you approach the driver's door and pushing you into his vehicle. Why take the risk; it might be innocent. It also might be a mugging setup.

If you are going to your car and you see a big van parked on the driver's side, it is recommended that you get in the passenger side door and slide over. Yes, it may feel a little funny and be quite awkward, but it is safe. Statistically, kidnappings happen as a guy jumps out of the sliding door of his van and pushes you into the car, slamming the van door.

When you leave your car, write down your parking location on the ticket. One of the worst things you can do is be lost and run up and down aisles looking for your car.

Have your keys out when you walk to your car. If you have to look down while fumbling in your purse for your keys, you look like a victim who is not paying attention to what is happening around you. The position is an invite if a man waiting for someone vulnerable. Go to your car, slide in quickly, and immediately lock the door. Now, drive away. People who get in their car and then make calls from the smartphones, door their checkbook, or a myriad of other activities with the engine off, are (statistically speaking) considerably raising their risk level.

When you get out of your car heading to the store, take a minute to note where the exits are. Also, scan the area for strange men loitering around for no apparent reason. If you see such a person, either get back in your car and drive to a different parking spot or choose a different entrance and pathway to walk. Again, you are just reducing the odds, and it is so simple.

With a baby in one hand, a package in the other you are vulnerable and men know it. You need to take extra precautions when you are in that situation. If you are at the grocery store, put the food cart behind you, so it acts as a sort of barrier to anyone approaching. Put your groceries in first. There are two ways to put your baby in, once all the groceries are in the car. The first is to look around carefully, put the baby in the car seat while keeping a careful eye out for approaching strangers. The other is to climb in the back seat with the baby, lock the doors, and put the baby in the car seat. Then get out and jump into the front seat locking the door. All you are really doing is putting the most valuable in last, and keeping vigilant so you do not look like a victim.

Another easy and constructive concept is to realize when cars are parked next to each other, side-by-side, it is easy for someone to duck down and be hidden. That person can then jump up when you approach. Instead, have your keys out, and look down the narrow lane before you enter. Also, many keyless cars have key fobs that either hunk your horn or lock your vehicle sounding the horn. You might keep your finger on that button as you near your car.

It is the opposite of how you were probably raised, for there is a natural inclination to help strangers who ask questions or seem lost. Statistically speaking, male attackers often ask for: (a) help, (b) the time, (c) directors how to find some store, or

(d) anything to make you stop and face them. It is a sad truth and a horrible commentary on our society that a woman alone is better off ignoring the person and not answering his question. It is rude, but most importantly, it is a safe way.

Finally, be reluctant to take the stairs; use the garage elevator. Garage stairs tend to be infrequently used, isolated, muffled sound, and are sometimes dark. Statistically higher than average muggings occur in stairs than other parts of the garage. As you take the elevator, step back after pressing the button, so you are immediately next to the doors as the elevator opens. Look who is inside before stepping into the elevator, and trust your gut. If you feel unsure of the situation, just tell the man you are waiting for your boyfriend who is parking your car and do not get in the elevator.

Walking Alone

If it is a route you will often be taken, make the acquaintance with the people and business owners along the way. Smile and greet them every time you pass. They can become a safety net for you and will look out for you as you walk past them.

If possible wear shoes you can run in. Take off your high heels and carry them in your purse as you put on flat surface shoes. You need to be free to run in an emergency and, it is tough to run in the wrong shoes.

Walk in the middle of the sidewalk, not right next to the building where people could theoretically reach out from doorways and grab you. At corners do not cut the angle short, but walk wide so you can see around the corner before you make the full turn. Basically, ignore strangers and do not talk to people who ask you questions or make comments as you walk down the street, head held high. Smiling in an open and friendly way and talking to anyone invites strangers to get close to you, which is the opposite of what you are trying to accomplish.

If you are walking down a long road with few people and businesses, walk facing traffic so you can see approaching cars. If you walk, travel the same way as traffic. Otherwise, you cannot see anyone approaching you from behind in a car.

Walking Alone at Night

You may have taken the train from work or for whatever reason need to walk home at night alone, which can be especially concerning if the streets are dimly lit. Besides the advice above, also try to stick to well-lit streets with people on them. That says you do not take shortcuts through parks or dark alleys. If you can afford it, take a cab. Consider cell phone apps (applications) where you coordinate with friends or family, so they expect your text that you arrived safely, and if not, to phone the police.

Flat Tire in Car

If you are stopped by the road because your vehicle has a flat tire, or the motor stopped running, you would appreciate nothing more than a man stopping by to help you. In years past, such behavior would be very reasonable. Unfortunately, read the newspaper, and you find that statistically, such trusting behavior exposes you to risk. It is sad but true.

The safer alternative, assuming you do not have access to a working cell phone, is when someone stops to help you, lock your doors. Then, just roll down the window a little. Then tell the person to please phone AAA (American Automobile

Association) or whatever roadside assistance you have, or just to phone the highway patrol.

Man with a Gun Demands Your Purse

This is simple, just give him your purse. But, instead of handing it over, throw it over in the bushes or ten feet from you in the other direction. As he zips towards your purse, you run the other way. Ideally, you should always have $20 stashed elsewhere on your person so you can take a cab home or to the police.

You should already have copies of every credit card and identification in your wallet to cancel your credit cards and alert your bank immediately. You can put a fraud alert through the three major credit agencies. When you report the crime to the police, they should give you directions on how to proceed. It is all replaceable, although it is a headache, but you are safely out of harm's way and able to personally deal with the issues.

Date Rape Drugs

Parties can be a lot of fun, but they can also be a high-risk endeavor if you do not take necessary precautions. Statistically, most rapes are done by someone you know. It is a sad commentary on our society that so many women are raped because someone put something in their drink. You need to protect your glass as if your sanity depends on it since indeed it might.

The most popular date rape drug, GHB, is easy to make in a chemistry lab and apparently is sold over the Internet. GHB is odorless, colorless, and tasteless, and it has a sedative effect rending you incapable of controlling yourself and making any decisions. News reports stated these women felt like they were like a zombie with no will-power at all. Worse, when they wake up the next day, these women have no memory of the past hours, so they often cannot even say what happened or even if they had sex while unconscious.

Police say it is relatively easy to buy GHB over the Internet. Worse, yet, for some reason, certain people seem to think it is all right and very acceptable to date rape a semi-conscious woman.

One common technique of adding GHB to your drink is called *palming*. You hold your hand parallel to the floor. You put a GHB pill (discussed below) in your hand, between your little finger and your thumb. Both fingers are covered by the back of your hand. Now, as the rapist reaches for the drink, he releases his fingers, and the GHB drops into your glass. The total time takes about ten seconds, and you can not see anything suspicious.

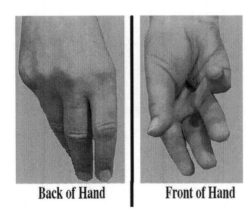

Back of Hand | **Front of Hand**

GHB is the most significant date rape drug, but Roofies (Rohypnol), ketamine, and other drugs can have similar effects. It is your life and your body. You owe it to yourself to do some basic Internet research and find out a little more about the use and effects of these drugs. I also recommend that you investigate what to do if you think you have ingested such a drug and felt you been date raped while on a drug. The time to gain knowledge is before anything happens, not afterward.

It is so easy for one to put something into your drink, and then if you finish your drink, it may be too late to do anything. Remember, all it takes is a few seconds to drop something in your glass.

Do not put your drink down for a minute. If you do rest in on the table, <u>do not</u> pick it back up to drink. Spill it out and go get a new drink. If your date brings you a drink unless you know the man well and trust him fully, just take the offering, pretend to take a sip, and then discard the glass. Now, go get yourself a new drink. Also, do not drink from punch bowls and open containers. If your drink tastes funny, or you are concerned about your drink, get a new one. Remember, you are seeking to lower the risk of getting raped. It is devastating, so undergo a little inconvenience and paranoia, and protect yourself.

Also, when you go to a party, write down on a piece of paper by your phone at home whom you are going with, his phone number, where the party is, and approximately what time you expect to be home. Never go to a party without your cell phone, fully charged, and extra cash for an emergency taxi.

Saying "No" Correctly

As a man, I am surprised at how many people really do not hear a woman say "no." But, then, unfortunately, so many women say "no" in ambiguous language that a man looking for "yes" can ignore the real message and focus on what he wants to hear. My father told me when I was a teenager a somewhat bad but far too true joke: "God gave man only enough blood to run his brain or his penis, but not enough to run both at the same time."

Most likely your upbringing included statements like: be nice, be tactful, and be pleasant. So, a woman who is not interested in a man might say: "Gee, you are a nice guy and all, but I am not looking for someone just now. Perhaps at another time." Worse, she may deliver this line while smiling, looking open and pleasant. Some men are dimwitted enough *not* to get the message.

When a woman says "no" today, it is better to be absolutely clear and unequivocal. Do not smile. Do not look happy. Do not act polite. Just act definite and say firmly: "I am not interested in you."

If you are being somewhat intimate with your date, and he does something you do not want, such as trying to take you to bed against your wishes, or some act that feels unappealing, tell him so in no uncertain terms. Say: "no, do not touch me" or "stop, I am not getting pleasure from this." If he continues, tell your date: "if you continue, I am leaving." Then, leave! Do not look back (mixed message); do not look for him across the room (mixed message). Make yourself firm, even if you are not comfortable being rigid.

Attack Speech

If the aggressor still does not get the message, try to leave. If he follows you, go to anybody else and tell them that this guy (and point directly at him) is stalking you and making you uncomfortable. Say it loudly so many people can hear you. Then, ask your new listener if he can make the aggressor go away and leave you alone. Most people are only just too happy to do so if your speech has not already made the aggressor go away.

Understand that you are under attack. This is more than some guy just making you embarrassed. This situation has the potential to escalate. It is you or him.

When you realize that he is attacking you psychologically, you should be willing to embarrass yourself just a little by crying for help and greatly embarrassing him. Alternatively, you can ask in a loud voice if your "new friend" would phone the police for you. That definitely will dislodge most attackers.

Final Words

So many self-defense books start out showing you how to counter a punch or a grab. That is putting the cart before the horse. You should be able to talk yourself out of or avoid seventy to ninety percent of the situations where you might need ju-jitsu or karate. That is why this book spends so much time on the "before attack" situations and why you should study carefully how to avoid potentially dangerous situations.

Chapter 12

If You Think
You Are Being Followed

If you think you might be followed by somebody, you are already a big step ahead. Assume for a minute it is true. That means you have time to prepare for your attacker. It also says you have an opportunity to discourage your potential attacker and have him leave you alone. But, the first step is to try and ascertain if, in fact, the person is really following you.

Ascertain if Person Following You

It may be difficult to verify with absolute certainty that someone is following, but still, you can determine that someone is probably watching you. That should be sufficient for your needs. Follow your instinct and assume the man is following you.

Followed on a Sidewalk

There are sure signs that usually allow you to conclude that you are being followed. Probably the biggest revealing clue is if the person is matching you step for step. By that, I mean if someone is following you and he walks slow when you walk slow and speeds up when you speed up. Try taking small steps, almost like baby steps. If he is really following you and does not want to pass you, he will have to make small steps. Someone matching your steps is likely following you. Some people cross to walk on the other side of the road, but that may not be a clear indication as he could still be following you while just walking on the other side of the street. Turning the corner may also help, but, again, the clearest indications are that person is matching your stride.

If you have a hand mirror take it out and look behind you to study the person. Or, use the reflection of store windows to see behind you. If there a taxi nearby, get in and go two blocks and get out. If the person is still there, then he is following you.

Sometimes you may think a man is following you, but you are not sure because he seemed to have a different color shirt or a new hat on. However, it is not uncommon for someone with a little training to know how easy it is to put on a jacket, add a cap, turn a shirt inside out to a different color to look different. One trick is to look at his shoes. Are they polished? What color are they? How many laces or what type of buckle or style is the man wearing? People may change a jacket or shirt, but they very rarely bother bringing an extra pair of shoes to change into.

Another sign is if the person looks at you and tries to stare you down. The average person avoids eye contact, and if he is a stranger with no interest in you, he tends to look elsewhere when you stare at him directly into his eyes. Not so for someone who is following you. In fact, such direct eye contact is sometimes a sign that something is going to happen soon.

Followed in Store

If you are in a store and you think someone may be following you, go to locations where men do not ordinarily go. For example, if you are in a department store, walk up to the woman's lingerie department, then meander down to the cooking section, and go to woman's purses and handbags. If the person ends up in all three departments, you can be reasonably sure he is following you.

In that case, walk to any store employee and ask for help. They can call for help, or at least a manager should confront the individual. Do not wait and hope he goes away. Do not be timid about asking for help and describing the man as best you can. Even conspicuously point the person out in such a way as he can see you. That will often discourage someone.

Followed in Car

If you are driving and you think you are being followed, the first test is to slow down and see if the suspect car also slows down. I took a class once on "Type A/Type B Behavior" by famed cardiologist Meyer Friedman, and the first task he had us do was to drive in the slow lane for a whole week. Believe me, it is hard to slow down to a crawl when you are Type A.

After going slow for a while, try speeding up and turning a corner to see if the car stays with you. Remember, a car following you might well drop a car or two behind you while trailing you to make it more difficult to ascertain if you are being followed.

Next, if you are on surface roads, make four right-hand turns going around the block. Almost nobody just drives around the block for pleasure. On the freeway, get off and then get back on the same highway. See if they are following.

If you are walking and you think a car might be following you while you are walking, turn around and walk the other way. If the vehicle is following you, it will have to turn around. Take a picture of the license plate and send it to a friend. Then call the police.

If Followed on Foot

Let Him Know You Are Aware of Him. If you believe the person is following you, be in heighten alert mode, and turn around and stare directly at him. Statistically, about half the people who may be following you will walk the other way if they think they are found out. Why I do not know, but I guess they feel a confident stare is a challenge, and such men maybe are looking for easy prey. If that is not enough, ask them in a firm voice: "are you following me?" Many people will mumble something and slitter away. Some will not and may even say, "Yes, I am following you."

Ask for Help. Your next step is to walk where there are people. Then ask for help. Just yelling, "I am scared of this man. Please call the police." This might not motivate others to get involved. Instead be more direct and try to engage a particular person.

> Instead say: "You sir, in the red shirt. That man is following me, and I am afraid of him. You look like you would help your daughter or your relative. Will you please help me? Please, please, call 911, which is the police, and give them my location. Also, please describe the man I am afraid of."

Very likely, the direct plea to a specific man will motivate him to help. If not, ask the next person, and so on until you get help.

Face Your Attacker. It is always better to have witnesses. So, if all else fails, and nobody will call the police or get involved, and the man is staying, then you just have to face him. If you have a weapon, like a pen, newspaper, belt, or whatever, get it. Take a ready stance and tell the man to leave you alone. Do not say, "please." Stare at him and do not reveal your secret that you know self-defense. Let him be unaware of how powerful you are.

Alternatively, you might try taking his picture and phoning the police. Although if you do so, be on heightened alert for his attack. If you do phone the police, try to describe the man. Not so much about his clothes, as about his weight, height (guess as opposed to your height), age, eye color, hair, is he clean or dirty, and other attributes.

If Followed in a Car

Stay Calm and On Good Streets. First, take several deep breaths and try to stay calm and think the situation through. Be sure all your windows are rolled up and, your doors are all locked. You do not want to take a chance that someone could jump in your car if it is momentarily stopped a stop sign or stoplight. Stay on well light, well-traveled roads. It is the dark alleys and long country roads that are the greatest danger. Never stop and get out of your car.

At stoplights, do not pull right behind the car in front of you. Leave about three or four feet, so if you need to, you can drive around the car in front to make an escape. It also prevents you from being sandwiched in by the car behind you. Unfortunately, it is a trick some attackers use if two people are following you in a car. They squeeze you into the car in front of you, and the passenger jumps out of the car and hops in your passenger side door, often breaking the window as he does so.

Get the License Plate. Try to get the license plate of the suspect car by looking in the rear-view mirror, or if you cannot do that, then try to ascertain some description of the car. Try taking a picture of the vehicle out your window, letting the person behind you see you taking the picture. That action might discourage him.

Call the Police. Phone 911 on your cell phone, if you can. If you contact the police, they will tell you what to do. Usually, they will direct you to the nearest police station. If driving is taking all your concentration, drive to the nearest police station and park. Generally, the suspect will not stop, but if he does, stay in the car and blow your horn. A policeman will come outside.

I do not advise going home because while the car probably will not stop in front of your house, he will know where you live. Drive to a hospital, a fire station, or other public places with lots of people and seek help. Remember, stay in your car if you can and blow the horn until help comes. If all else fails, drive to a friend's house and call the police from there.

Chapter 13

Stay Safe in Nightclubs and Hookups

A single woman going to a bar or nightclub these days can be a risky adventure. It is sad but true. The purpose of this chapter is to give you the advice to reduce your risk level; it is not to say that if you follow all the information you are safe. Nobody can promise that.

I realize in setting forth these avenues of self-preservation that some or all suggestions may be ignored. In my teenage years, when I was young and dumb and full of hubris, I often skied down mountains I had no business descending. Fortunately, I wasn't injured, and it was always the "other guy" who broke a leg. My risk level was so high I look back now and wonder how I could've been so blinded and able to ignore reality totally.

I urge you not to make similar mistakes or to skip the probabilities that a single woman faces by going to a nightclub. As the first chapter explained, at least one in five women will be raped or attacked during her lifetime. Further, sadistically speaking, if you are under 35, your risk or higher than those over 35. Of course, it is unfair, but you can't afford to be naive and ignore the statistics. It is a matter of how much do you want to reduce your chance of being attacked. The advice is common sense, and some of it comes from the San Francisco police department criminal rape section. Finally, for convenience, I am using nightclub as a synonym for a traditional nightclub, bar, or restaurant with a bar on the side.

Before leaving the house.

Tell Others Your Destination

Let others know you are going out. I recommend telling at least one other person and possibly two, that you were going out for the night to the XYZ night club, and should be home by 12:30 AM. If you are not, and you have not called, they should be concerned. If you are kidnapped and raped and dumped bleeding in a back alley, who would know and for how many days could you live there before someone became concerned?

Go in Groups

The old adage that there is safety in numbers is never so true as when you go to a nightclub. You should go with at least one other person, and preferably two others.

Phone Fully Charged

Make sure your phone is fully charged so it will be available if you need it in an emergency.

Back Up Written Numbers

If your phone is stolen or lost, often inside your purse, if that is taken, who can you phone and who's number do you know by heart. It may be easier for a woman working and living in an apartment, but it is especially imperative for college students and people new to the city, do you have such information. It is advisable to write two or three numbers down on a piece of paper.

Carry Cash in Your Shoe

I would also recommend sticking a $20 bill or whatever amount will ensure cab fare home in your shoe with the phone numbers. If your purse, wallet, and phone are taken, at least you will have cab fare back.

Keep Your On-Line Life Private

Don't rush to put on the social media that you are going to or are at XYZ club. It sounds incredible, but I occasionally hear about a woman who posts a statement that she is at XYZ club, drunk, and having a grate time. Never advertise, because sadly in today's world, you never know who is scanning internet entries.

Evaluate Before Entering

Parking Your Car

If you are driving, which is not always wise if you're going to be drinking, try not to park in either a dark alley or immediately in front of the club. They throw drunks and violent offenders out the front door, and some remain to loiter nearby looking for trouble.

Pick a Good Nightclub

You can get some feeling for night club just by looking at the entrance, neighborhood, and sidewalk. If people are just milling about and gathering at the front door, as opposed to standing in a line, it suggests the controls inside over the patrons maybe lax as well. If the front entrance is well lit and clean, it helps detour risky behavior. If you see security cameras, it suggests the club is serious about security. Such factors are not a guarantee, but just a features to consider and evaluating your risk as a single woman entering the establishment.

Doorman at Front Door

Consider if there a bouncer or security guard at the entrance checking ID, and padding down people who look like they might be caring a weapon. IF there is a doorman, does he or she just let anybody in without any attempt to evaluate the potential customers? A good attendant is a hallmark of a safer environment.

Inside the Nightclub

Don't Flash Cash

Don't pull out a wad of bills in a nightclub to pay your tab. It invites a robbery. Pay by credit card or have some small bills in a separate part of your purse.

Don't Get Drunk

People who have too much to drink and become drunk, lose much of their judgment and impair their common sense. Everyone has their own limit. If you don't know yours, the Canada drinking guidelines suggest you set a limit and stick to them. They suggest you drink slowly, alternate alcoholic and nonalcoholic drinks and eat before and while drinking. They also recommend an adult woman have not more than three drinks. If you want to get drunk, do it at home or at a friends house. Being drunk in a nightclub increases your risk level.

Prevent Date Rape Drug

This topic is important so I am covering the subject of a previous chapter, but with new material. Intentional drugging is one of the most important and preventable topics you can follow in a nightclub.

Unfortunately, one of the problems a woman face is someone depositing a date rape drug into their drink. Many studies have shown how surprisingly easy and quick it is to drop a pill undetected into a woman's glass. One scientific paper (390 patients during 2013-2014 reported by UCSF doctor L.A. Richer in 2015) stated that over half the raped patients studied were victimized using a date rape drug.

It's relatively easy to reduce the risk of getting drugged, by holding your glasses at all times. Many people recommend keeping your hand over the top of the glass, and I leave it to you to decide if that is overkill. If you ever put your glass down, I recommend *always* buying a new drink. It only takes two seconds to drop a pill in your glass, so for a few dollars why take the risk. I also would be careful about excepting a drink from a man who approaches you, especially if you have not seen the drink being made. Any drink should be given directly to you from the bartender.

From a long list of date rape drugs, the most common are GHB ("liquid ecstasy"), Rohypnol ("roofies'), and ketamine ("Special K"). These drugs make you unable to resist rape and often cause retrograde amnesia so you can't remember what happened. Regardless of the date-rape drug used, the critical fact is that such drugs exist, are easy to obtain, and are used far too often to ignore their existence.

Although they are generally tasteless in an alcoholic drink, the most common side-effect is feeling suddenly very drunk and light-headed, even though you may not have much or anything of your beverage.

If you have those feelings, you should immediately call 911 and tell them where you are and that you think you've been drugged. Tell the bouncer, doorman, or manager the same and ask him or her to make sure you don't leave with a stranger and are turned over the paramedics or police. Since you might be unconscious at any moment, don't waste time; act immediately. Naturally, don't drink any more of your drink.

Note the Exits

Safety is more than just preventing an attack. When you enter the club, it is highly advisable to take notice of the various exits. In the event of a fire, shooting, or big brawl in the club, you may need a quick exit. In 2016 in Oakland, California (on the other side of the Bay Bridge from San Francisco) there was a fire at the "Ghost Ship" nightclub. A total of 36 people were killed in the blaze, the deadliest in the history of Oakland, and according to Wikipedia, the most fatal fire in California since the 1906 San Francisco Earthquake and Fire.

Don't Antagonize Bouncers

It would seem obvious that a woman should not antagonize or demean the doorman or the bouncers. Yet, a certain number of women seem to do that every night. Most bouncers are well trained to eject you in a gentle manner. However, because the pay is low and the work dangerous, there are always some bouncers who don't take kindly to being "dumped on." They might eject you while inflicting damage they cannot be seen. Don't risk it.

Leave by Midnight

Statistically speaking, a woman is more at risk after midnight. That is not to say that before midnight is safe, only that the probability goes up after midnight. Consider leaving the club before 12:00 AM. Remember any guy you pick up in the early morning is more likely to be a heavy drinker, and for some the more one drinks the more dangerous they become.

Be Aware of Surroundings

Keep an open eye out for what is going on around you. If you someone at the bar is loudly yelling at a woman or arguing with a guy, it could escalate into a fight. Learn to recognize a potentially risky situation and consider if it might be time to find another nightclub.

Picking a Friend for the Night

Use Date Sense

There are far better books than this one on how to select dates, but I suggest being apprehensive about a guy who doesn't take "no" for an answer. Some psychologists claim such behavior is a form of dominate control from a potentially dangerous person.

You should also be somewhat hesitant about leaving the nightclub with a guy, but if you must, then tell another in your group or phone a friend where you are going and who you are leaving with. The best advice is the "listen to your gut." If it doesn't feel right, it probably isn't an acceptable risk.

Leaving the Nightclub

Walk with Confidence

You need to walk with your head held high, your eyes scanning the area, with straight posture, and a normal stride. Rapists generally pick targets that are distracted (e.g., women talking on a cell phone or searching in their purse for the keys), or that look timid and scared. Pretend you are on a movie set and act the part.

There are many ways to deveope a confident walk. If you are unsure how to proceed, one method if power walking. Google "power walking," and walk for a few hours (ten minutes a day is fine). Once you have the technique memorized, slow the place to a normal walking speed, using the power walking body positions and actions.

Purse on Other Shoulder

Put your purse on your non-dominant shoulder. In other words, if you are right-handed, carry your purse over your left shoulder. You need your strong arms to fight off an attacker.

My advice is if someone wants your wallet, give it to man. Items, identification and the like can be replaced, but broken bones or stab wounds don't heal well. Besides, your purse should be basically empty, with little cash, your driver's license, a medical card, and your credit card. The credit card should be one that has a low budget amount, say $250.

Speak in a Strong Tone

If someone is approaching you need to make a comment in a robust, firm voice. You might say something like, "oh, I thought you were my boyfriend and his friends who are already late picking me up." Whatever you chose to tell, don't squeak it out in a stuttering voice. Speak powerfully and firmly, and to be able to do that, it is advisable to practice speaking into a mirror at home.

Don't Walk Home Alone

Walking home at night alone is a gamble with dire consequences if you guess wrong. Spend the money and take a taxi or other means of transportation. According to some cops, the riskiest part is that someone might follow you home a half-block back on the other side of the street, then nab you just as you are putting your keys in the door.

If you expect to be walking home, you might carry a Taser or other non-lethal weapon in your purse, and have it in your hand during your walk.

People are split on the use of Mace. I'm on the side that doesn't recommend it, because if the wind is blowing in the wrong way, you might get Mace in your face. Additionally, you must be close enough to spray your attacker without being caught, which might be difficult for the untrained. In other words, you have to let the attacker get close enough to you before you can spray him.

Talk to the police if you want a weapon and don't know which kind would be best for you. Alternatively, talk to rape crisis counselors or Google suggestions from victims of rape.

In Bed and You Don't Want Sex

Introduction

Chapter 11 (Reduce the Risks in Your Life) discussed how to say "no" when not wanting to go out with somebody. This chapter goes further, and discusses how to say "no" when you already in bed with that person.

Why Say No

There are many reasons that you might not want to have sex with someone, even though you are in bed together. Perhaps he is pushing you for sex without adequate concern for you, or refusing to wear a condom, or for whatever reason, it just doesn't feel right. Always trust your gut.

Say No Firmly

First pull back the sheets (in the unlikely and unfortunate event you have to physically prevent a rape). Then tell your hook up "can we stop fror a minute, because you have something to tell him. It is more effective talking when he is not gengaged in sex. So "no" firmly, directly and correctly, in no ambigious terms.

Then try and get up to dress and leave. If he doesn't, then try reminding the man of the facts of rape. Tell him your friends know you are here and the address, and if you don't call in within the hour, they have been instructed to report it to the police. Remind the man that when you leave, since nothing happened, he is a free man, but if he tries to rape you, he will end up in jail. Then ask if it worth a jail sentence.

Probably the most notorious case where the "facts of life"

can save you in 2014 when the professional mixed martial arts [ju-jitsu and karate] fighter Jonathan Koppenhaver broke into his ex-girlfriend's unit in Las Vegas and began beating her and her boyfriend. After being beaten almost senseless, the boyfriend, Corry Thomas, look at the attacker and said, "You gotta kill me, or you gotta let me go." At that point, Koppenhaver fled the scene. (He is now serving 36 years to life in prison.) Such logic does work.

San Francisco police officer Roberts was a guest speaker at one of my woman's self-defense classes. He suggested telling the guy his breath smells of bad alcohol and he should brush his teeth first. When the guy leaves for the bathroom, grab your clothes and purse, run out the door, and put your clothes on outside the unit. Another solution he suggested is to tell him you have gonorrhea. Roberts also recommend you might mention having AIDS, and you were going to say nothing, but your conscience won't let me have sex without telling you. I have mixed feeling on that last piece of advice because the guy might be mad thinking you have just infected him, even though you haven't yet had sex.

Physically Fighting Back

Fighting is always the very last resort, and you might get hurt. If it is important enough, then attack with fury and don't give up. If you haven't already, try to pull off the covers before you begin fighting. Read the chapter on "Obnoxious Hookups in the Car," as well as the second half of this book

Chapter 14

Protecting Yourself at Home

Living alone in your own apartment or home can be very liberating, but it can still be a little intimidating and frightening at times. Like so much of self-defense, it is a matter of balancing the risks versus the costs (emotionally or economically) of reducing those risks. No matter how careful you become or how much you spend on home security, you can never be 100% safe. Fortunately, if you follow the five rules of safety suggested by most police departments and make them into habits, you can be reasonably safe.

Rule One: Answering the Front Door

Whether or not to answer the door is one of the most challenging issues for many single people. When the person on the other side begs to let him in to call the car company for a towing, or a woman crying that someone is chasing her, there is a natural human kindness to want to help. Don't do it, there are ways to help without letting the person in.

Peek at Them

The very first thing you should do is look through the peephole to see if it's one or more people and how the person looks. When you are alone, you can never take the risk of not looking through the door to see who it is before opening your home.

Call Out to Fictitious Friend

It's not a bad idea to immediately say it loudly, "it's OK Billy, I'll get the door," or "turn down the eggs, Joe, I'll just get the door." All of these are designed to imply you are not alone. Sometimes that is enough to deter a burglar.

Let Them Know You Are Home

There are two schools of thought. I prefer to let the stranger know you are home and not interested. Some people prefer to pretend they're not home and do not answer. If the person is a burglar looking for an empty house, he might break in surprising you. Secondly, by not responding, he may come back later to try and find you when you are home.

One San Francisco police offer suggested taking a picture of the person through the peephole and letting the person know you have made the picture and have sent it to a friendly police detective you are dating. Such information will often deter many potential criminals because they can be identified as you have a relationship with the police.

Don't Open the Door

You are alone and never know if the other person is strung out on drugs or looking to burglarize your home to score his or her next fix. Remember that guns are often easier to find than liquor.

If the person says he needs to call a car service like AAA, tell him you will be happy to make the call if he gives you the number. Just do not let the person in. If the person claims to be running from someone who is chasing him or her, offer to call the police. Tell them they can stay on your front porch until the cops arrive. You are helping, but you are not crossing the line to excessive risk.

If you see a cop or a service repairman that you think might be legitimate, ask them to pass their identification under the door. They are used to this type of request. Then call the police station or service company to ask if they are legitimate and are entitled to be at your place of residence. It is often best to look up the phone number, and not use the phone number they give you unless it appears to be almost the same phone number as the one you were looking up.

Do not open the door figuring the chain on the door will protect you. That chain is only held in place by simple wood screws. All the other person has to do is push his body against the door with all his weight, and generally, the door opens, and you land flat on your back.

Don't Answer Personal Questions

If the person asks through the closed door where you work, what time you usually leave during the day, or anything personal that reveals details about you, you should not respond. He may be casing the joint for a future break-in. You don't want to give him any information to a perfect stranger.

For that matter, be careful about revealing too much about yourself to a neighbor and casual friends until you feel you know them well enough that they can be trusted with such information.

Don't Answer Personal Questions

If you are troubled or have that uneasy feeling in your gut that this is not a nice man, leave through the back door and go to a neighbor's house. Don't stay in your home alone. At the neighbors, call the police.

Rule Two: Get to Know Your Neighbors

Neighbors are some of the best protection you can have, and most importantly, they can provide a sense of companionship and care. It's not hard to meet your neighbors. Benjamin Franklin said it best when he claimed the best way to approach a difficult person, is to ask them to do you a favor. You could knock on the neighbor's door, introduce yourself, and ask them where they shop or what is best cleaners nearby.

Even if you find meeting people difficult, for the sake of your safety, you can reach out and establish contact. When you first meet people use caution about revealing too much about yourself. You don't have to be best friends with your neighbors, but you should be friendly and feel close enough that they know who you are and are comfortable with you.

Neighbors can keep a watch on your place if you go away for a weekend. They can also tell you if somebody is coming by during the day. Additionally, if you need help or are fearful of someone, they can offer sanctuary.

Rule Three: Keep Doors and Windows Locked

The idea of keeping your doors and windows locked sounds so obvious you wonder why it would be in a book. The answer is easy. Far too often doors were left unlocked, and some windows are even left open. Needless to say, such a situation invites unscrupulous visitors to take advantage of an open opportunity.

Develop a Routine

You should have a regular routine that you practice daily until it becomes an automatic habit. Start from one end of the house and go through each room, the same way each night, checking the doors and windows to make sure they are locked. Some do thhis more than once a day because it takes so little time; others do not.

Drapes and Venetian Blinds

An open window allows anyone to look in and see your type of furniture and furnishings, and most importantly, to note that you are living alone. Close the drapes and keep them closed if possible.

Venetian blinds should be kept closed, with a slight opening facing up towards the ceiling. In other words, you should be able to look out the shades and see the grounds. Upstairs, on the second story, you would close the blinds the opposite way. Now when you look out, you view the sky. Anyone outside your building is looking up at the second story only sees the ceiling and not parts of you.

If You Must Open a Window

If The weather is hot, and you don't have an air-conditioner, try and open the upstairs windows (provided they are safe and inaccessible) and keep the downstairs closed. If you must open the downstairs window, only open them about six inches, preventing someone from slipping inside. To do so, you will need a wooden dowel or broomstick cut to size or special locks to prevent the window from being forced open. There is more about locks later in this chapter.

Upstairs windows must be clear of hanging tree branches, trellises with climbing plants, low hanging balconies, and other objects that allow someone to reach or climb to the second story easily. It is not worth opening an upstairs window, even part way if someone can quickly scale up to it.

Rule Four: Maintain Decent Locks

If you carefully lock your doors, but the lock is so old, or the door fits so poorly, that anyone can push against the door to open it, your locks are worthless.

Adequate Locks

If you can afford it, invest in a decent deadbolt lock above your existing door lock. If money is not an issue, consider the new electronic locks, which allow you entry and will enable you to assign personal codes to other individuals such as cleaning ladies or houseguests.

If you can't afford a new lock, get a 2" x 4" board, and I have a friend or handyman secure it to the door as a crossbar. The cost of the materials is probably less than $20. If you are not sure if your locks are adequate, many police departments will send an officer to stop by at a convenient time to walk through your place and make suggestions.

Re-Key Locks

It might be a wise idea to re-key the locks. A locksmith can easily add a pin or modify an existing pen so old keys will not work, and many times the cost is not too expensive. If you are comfortable enough to unscrew the locks and have a friend who can stay in your unit until you return, you can take the locks to the locksmith's shop where you will not be paying the cost of transportation to your home.

Sliding Glass Doors

Sliding glass doors are always a problem. They are not as secure as they seem, and the regular lock is not tamperproof. The first thing to do is to put a broomstick or dowel in the sliding track when you close the door to make it harder to jimmy open. Alternatively, a better option is to buy a particular keyed patio door lock the bolts into the sliding track. Finally, the actual lock on the sliding door can be improved by a "sliding door loop-lock" (or sometimes called a "J-Lock").

If you are looking for greater security on a sliding door, you can get small wireless alarms that attach to the glass door. They signal if the door is being opened, or if the door is vibrating as if someone is trying to break in.

Windows

You will also need to check each window to make sure it has a secure locking mechanism that works. If not, you need to secure the window with a new lock. As I mentioned before, if you are going to leave the window partly open, but still narrow enough that anybody can slip through, you will need a wood dowel or window lock that will secure a partially open window. If your windows are old and weak, you can purchase a security film that you apply which strengthens your windows. According to the advertising, if you hit the window with a hammer, it cracks like a front car windshield but does not break. Security film makes it harder to enter, but like everything else, a determined burglar can get in eventually.

Rule Five: Don't Advertise You Live Alone

For your own safety, you never want to advertise that you live alone. So, for example, if you live in an apartment, don't put a sign on your mailbox or buzzer entry that says, "Jane Doe." Instead put a sign that says, "Jane Doe and family," or "Doe Residence." One police officer suggested college students living alone might want to put something like, "J. Doe and Roger Smith." I'm not sure how I feel about the last option, but it sure does camouflage the fact that you live alone.

Similarly, many people live on the Internet. From a pure safety point of view, don't advertise you're going on vacation or that you live alone.

Guns for Protection

You can probably have as many different opinions about guns as they are leaves on a tree. If you go on the Internet, you will find enough information to make an informed decision. **Personally, I don't recommend a gun**, because too many people lack the training and emotional ability to fire **immediately** at an intruder. They hesitate and cause the burglar to fire first. Additionally, as reported in the newspapers, too often the gunman ends up shooting a neighbor or family member. I think a gun is useless unless you are willing to train properly.

If you are going to get a weapon, unlike most people, I recommend a short barrel shotgun. It's not that a shotgun is so much more useful than a pistol because at the small distance of a room your pallet spread is narrow. Instead, the benefit is that people have an easier time psychologically pulling the trigger, and the psychological effect of facing such a gun is frightening to many burglars who might just have a pistol.

Pistol Use in Real World

The New York Police Department did an important study of shootings involving police officers over ten years. You are probably 5 feet and many inches. According to this ten-year study or real world shootings, only 20% of the people who shot at a cop were able to hit a policeman at six feet away.

Far too often you grab a pistol in an emotional rush, and you fit the gun in the crook of your hand. However, with the adrenaline flowing the study found people tend to shoot based on where their forefinger would be pointing. It is like shooting pool if you're off an eighth of an inch with the pool cue (stick) when you hit the ball, by the time the ball gets to the other end of the pool table you can be off by six inches or more.

So, it is with a pistol, and even if you can take a shoot at an intruder at ten feet, statistically you only have a 10%-15% chance of hitting the intruder.

Using a Shotgun

The most frequent criticisms of a shotgun are that if you go around the corner, the shotgun goes first and that it takes two hands to hold a shotgun. With both hands busy, you can't carry a flashlight or call the police while holding a shotgun.

My approach is you never should be walking around your house looking to confront an intruder. I would recommend staying in your bedroom, or whatever room you feel is the safest, with the shotgun at the Ready position. First, you should have called the police from your room.

If you are holed up in a room, I would recommend turning the lights on. If you fire a weapon in the dark, the muzzle flash can be momentarily binding usually making a second shot very inaccurate.

You can buy shotgun bullets (pellets) that will not penetrate the walls. A serious disadvantage of shooting a pistol inside a home is the concept of "over-penetration" where the bullet misses the intruder and travel through walls and can hit someone two to three rooms away. Most interior walls in a house are just drywall (sometimes called wallboard), which is generally a half-inch thick sheet of plaster covered by paper. Drywall which hardly slow down a pistol or rifle round. This disadvantage may be of less concern to someone living alone.

Need Appropriate Training

Any gun, pistol, rifle, or shotgun will be fairly useless unless you go to the gun range and take lessons to learn how to use the weapon. Secondly, and this is my opinion, having qualified as an expert in the M16 while in the army, you must practice shooting targets of people and not bull's-eyes. Finally, after you are somewhat proficient, use realisitc photograph targets of real people. You need to desensitize yourself so that if you see an intruder you can fire before he does and your shot will be controlled and accurate.

If you do see an intruder and upon seeing your shotgun and if he is standing there like a deer in the headlight, you might want to tell him to carefully put down his gun, then turn around and leave the house. Without their gun, most intruders will likely leave the house.

Secure Room

Finally, if you do have a secure room that you will use, keep an old cell phone in that room, so it is always available. Most phones will call 911 or the police without a plan. In my opinion, a better idea if you hear somebody sneaking around is to have an exit strategy from your home and phone the police from a neighbor's house.

Buying a Pistol

People who don't like the idea of a shotgun ask what kind of pistol they should buy. My advice, which might differ significantly from others, is to buy a six-shot revolver. Why? Because it is so simple to use. These pistols are the guns you see in the "cowboy movies," where there is a revolving cylinder that holds six shots. Pull the trigger, and it shoots.

The other type of handgun, which apparently most professionals recommend, is the semi-automatic handgun. The gun carries more than six bullets in a magazine shoved into the handle of the gun. The weapon is supposed to fire every time you pull the trigger.

The problem is many people who keep a semi-automatic type of handgun in their home do not keep a live bullet in the chamber. Then, in the event of a situation, while under extreme pressure and adrenalin flowing, they go to fire at an intruder. Too often, they press the trigger, and nothing happens. The gun "dry fires," meaning there is no bullet to shoot. Instead, you would have had to "rack the slide" before you fire. To me, at least, I think there is too high a risk of misfire, and statistics do bear out that a certain percentage of people who attacked and have misfired the first shot.

As I mentioned at the beginning of the chapter if you are going to purchase a pistol, do your research and find someone you trust. There are a great many options on the types, size, and caliber of a handgun to purchase.

Miscellaneous Advice

There are many other things you can do to make yourself even safer, but the five tips above should be sufficient. However, if any of the suggestions below look appealing, consider adopting them.

Dogs

If you like pets almost everyone agrees that a barking dog scares away most burglars. They don't want to get caught, in the excited dog barking attract too much attention.

Internet and Family Protection

In the chapter on college freshman is a good section on using the Internet and family for protection. I recommend reading that portion of the chapter.

Letter for Repairs

If you live in an apartment and particular doors or windows are not secure, I would write the doorman or landlord about the problem, noting that a copy is also being sent to a friend or family member. Receiving such a message places the recipient in a somewhat awkward position because if anything happens to you, for insurance and liability purposes, they are on notice of a security risk in your unit. Some landlords seem to collect such notice, while others immediately make some repairs. You have nothing to lose by such a letter.

Landscaping

Try not to have any plants or object where an assailant could hide and sneak up on you. Cut down vegetation or trees that allow someone to conceal themselves, and plant cactus or thorny rose business near the house.

Alarm or Surveillance System

At one time, all alarm systems had to be hard-wired into the house, with wires goes from each window to a central arms box in your home. Today, all you need are some inexpensive wireless alarms units that are relatively inexpensive. You might consider adding them to doors and window if the price is reasonable.

Conversely, a surveillance system is a camera that potential intruders can see that takes pictures of anyone in the vicinity of that camera. It seems such systems significantly reduce the probability of a crime since burglars or rapists do not want to be recorded. Some studies say 50% reduction, and while I don't know the actual decrease, it is substantial.

Hiding Keys Outside

A good burglar can generally find a hidden key outside in fake rocks, under the doormat, above the door, in potted plants, or wherever you think is a safe hiding place. If you have to hide a second key, hide it maybe in a car or with a neighbor, but not outside your house. Yes, I know putting a key say in the trunk by the spare tire is not great, but in my opinion, it is better than hiding it outside your house.

More on Keys

If you ever lose your keys, you should immediately re-key the locks. Also, your key ring should not have any identification with it. Instead, attach a large purple heart or another symbol on your keyring so you can ask restaurants and friends if they found your keys.

Part Four

Pestering Attacks

Chapter 15

Introduction to Pestering Attacks

Of all the attacks, a pestering attack is one of the easiest to discourage. You are at a party when some man does not leave you alone. He is not physically attacking you, but verbally is insulting and almost stalking in his approach. You attempted to embarrass him telling his advances are not wanted, and he refused to take the hint when you asked in a loud voice for someone else to talk to him. The other situation is when the man is very drunk and at a party, making a pass and refusing to accept "no." Since verbal rebuffs are not working, even ones that would make most sober men blush, in both situations the only recourse is to do ju-jitsu.

Limits to Pain Resistances

It is essential to understand a man who is very drunk or high on drugs may not feel pain, and that makes your job harder. I taught members of the San Francisco police in extra classes of ju-jitsu, with emphasis on arresting and comealong techniques. I was far too often discomforted by the fact that my students reported they attempted to arrest somebody, but that a comealong moves that controlled someone by pain did not work.

In almost all cases the problem was the offender was drunk and therefore immune to pain control. Often the drunk would wake up sober with broken wrists or broken arms and had no recollection of how it happened. In short, pain control techniques are unreliable on a very drunk individual, and a different series of procedures are required.

I recommend a knuckle torture technique (rubbing your fingers in a fist against his knuckles to see if he reacts to pain) or any number of other methods (including a small jab to the ribs) to see if the person feels pain. If he does not react to torture, there is no use trying any technique that resorts to pain to control that man.

Also, there are a few, but not many men, who just naturally have a very high threshold for pain and are able to absorb an unusual amount of pain without moving. If you are ever in one of those rare situations, immediately stop the technique and switch to a more lethal or effective method.

Comealongs

Comealongs are joint techniques that hyper-extend a joint, or force that joint in a different direction, or threaten to break a joint if the person does not move the direction you indicate. The joints most commonly attacked are the finger, wrist, elbow, and ankle joints. Comealongs can cause considerable pain and are often used to subdue, control, injure, and/or arrest an attacker. Because you are using the weight and strength of your body to attack a single joint when correctly applied it is extremely hard to resist and fight against the technique. As such, comealongs are excellent moves for women against an attacker.

This book reviews three comealongs. The first two are the pain control type for sober men. The third comealong is for someone who is intoxicated or high on drugs and will not feel pain.

No Hip Throws

It is very common in ju-jitsu classes to see hip throws. You unbalance your opponent, pivot around, so your back is to his chest, lower your hip below his center of gravity. Then, you twist your body using the force of your entire body to rotate your attacker over your hip and flying to the floor in front of you. A more complex form of the throw is a shoulder throw when the opponent rotates around your shoulder instead of your hip but using a similar type of action as a hip throw. These throws are very effective; however, they take skill and practice to make them successful.

Since this book seeks to escape without lengthy training sessions, it would be self-defeating to employ hip throws when easier techniques are available. In another chapter, this book will use a small number of leg throws where a person is thrown to the ground over someone's leg, by reaping (sweeping out) the attacker's leg or thigh.

Chapter 16

Front Flex Comealong

(Sober or Slightly Drunk Person)

In this technique, the attacker grabs your outside wrist with his hand, so his knuckles are pointing outside of your body. Assume he grabs your left arm with his right hand. There are four steps to this technique.

Hitchhike Step. Make a fist. Now, from your elbow, rotate your arm in a circular motion, so your fist is now pointing skyward. It is almost like you are making a hitchhiking move. Your shoulder does not move. If your opponent

sees shoulder action, he may have time to react. Further, the effectiveness of this art is the circular movement pivoting at the elbow, which prevents his pectoral muscles from coming into play.

<u>Pry Free Step.</u> There should be a slight separation already visible between your wrist and the heal of his hand. Take your right arm and place your right thumb on the back of his knuckles of his hand. Now pry your left wrist from his grasp by working against the thumb. With that hand also grab his right hand, so both of your thumbs are against the back of his knuckles.

<u>90° Bend Step.</u> Now fully bend his wrist 90 degrees to his arm, and picture a brick wall from the floor to the ceiling running right through his hand. Raise his flexed wrist up and down that invisible wall. Do not go forward or backward, but go just up and down on a vertical plane.

<u>Break His Balance Step</u>. Push your attacker down, destroying his balance. Now if you want to move him in any direction, flex so his knees are bent, for as long as he is not straight, he cannot turn around and hit you or move easily. Note, that your back is relatively straight.

Optional Step - The Throw. To throw the attacker, should you so desire, step back with your left foot, using your entire body weight to turn his wrist towards and down near your left toe. He is forced to throw himself to the ground, or the attacker will break his wrist or dislocate his shoulder.

Switch Attacked Arm

After you have practiced and perfected this technique, practice it with him grabbing your other hand. After all, you can never be sure which wrist he will grab if he makes a wrist grip attack. After a short while, it shouldn't matter which arm he grabs. You should be equally comfortable on either side.

Practice Offensively

Next, practice this technique offensively. You need to be able to secure this hold if your attacker is just standing next to you with his arms at his sides.

Of course, this defense can be used from a great many different attack scenarios, but you are not learning for a belt in a ju-jitsu class. You only need to know how to apply this art in two positions.

Assume your attacker has his arms at the side as he stands across from you annoyingly. Step forward with your left foot, and

at the same time reach down with your left hand, your thumb towards the floor, as you grip the back of his hand.

Now just pivot and swing your arm up from the elbow and you are back in the same position as you were after breaking his wrist grip.

Chapter 17

Cross Twist Comealong
(Sober or Slightly Drunk Person)

This technique is called a cross twist comealong and is done from the same wrist grip as the front flex comealong. It can also be done if you go for a front flex comealong, but miss or are slowing down the move, and the attacker ducks under the arm to escape. Either way, he is in a perfect position for a cross flex comealong.

In this technique, the attacker grabs your outside wrist with his hand, so his knuckles are pointing outside of your body. Assume he grabs your left arm with his right hand.

Swing your arm in a wide circle up to the top. The secret is to make a wide

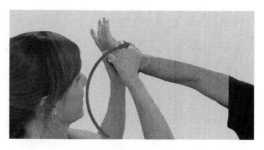

swing so your opponent cannot use his pectoral muscles to block or hinder the move.

When you grip your opponent's hand, your two thumbs either touch or cross on the back of his hand around the  middle knuckle. Your fingers wrap around his open hand tightly grabbing the flesh of his inside hand. This gives you a good tight grip from which he cannot escape.

Now, just continue twisting his hand in a circular motion to force him down to a position that has destroyed his balance and left him unable to escape.

He will now go wherever you command him because of the pain in his wrist if he does not come as directed.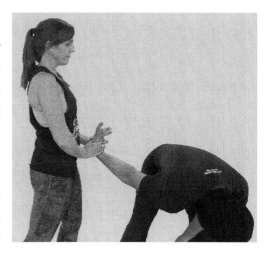

You can easily continue twisting his arm throwing him somersaulting onto his back or breaking his arm.

Switch Attacked Arm

After you have practiced and perfected this technique, practice it with someone grabbing your other hand. After all, you can never be sure which wrist the attacker will grab if he makes a wrist grip attack.

Offensive Attack

Next, practice this technique offensively. Your attacker has his arms at the side as he stands across from you annoyingly. Step forward with your left foot, and at the same time reach down and across your body with your right hand.

With your thumb towards the floor, as you grip the back of his hand.

Now just pivot and swing your arm up from your shoulder. You are back in the same position as you were after breaking the aggressor's wrist

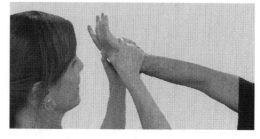

grip. Just continue on with the arm taking him down to the completed art, with his balance entirely destroyed.

Chapter 18

Straddle-Arm Comealong
(Very Drunk or Pain-Resistant Person)

This is the perfect comealong for a very drunk person. Remember, someone highly inebriated or high on drugs might not feel pain. This move can walk him out of the room, usually with everyone laughing at your opponent, causing him maximum embarrassment. More importantly, because it is so humorous to watch, none of the opponent's friends, if he has any at the party, are likely to intervene.

This technique gained considerable use by bouncers at bars in San Francisco who took our ju-jitsu classes. San Francisco police in the 1960s and 1970s used this technique when arresting someone from a situation where he might have had a lot of friends who could have intervened had he been taken away in handcuffs. With this art, few ever came to assist their "friend." I don't know, but it may still be used today. In any event, this is an excellent technique for a woman to remove an obnoxious individual from a party.

For unknown reasons, it seems women at first have a harder time with this art than other techniques. I am not sure why, since it is a simple move to employ. For that reason, this book contains additional photographs explaining the technique in greater detail.

When you are facing your opponent, the first thing you do is grab his outside wrist. Usually, if you are right handed, you use your right hand to grab his wrist.

Now pull his wrist straight down towards his toes. Do not move him forward, or he will just step and not bend forward at the waist. Also, do not pull down towards his ankles, as the attacker retains his center of gravity over his waist. Pull down towards the ends of his toes. (Note this picture shows the art from a different angle so, Angie is using her other hand. In practicing this art she would use her right hand.)

Now that the hand is down and his balance broken, push the hand towards the middle of his legs. Since your swing is at the end of his arm, the attacker's pectoral muscles cannot come into play and stop you. His arm moves surprisingly easily.

Step to his rear and push the attacker's arm between his legs. Do not be squeamish. It is just a move in furtherance of your self-defense.

Now, you switch hands. If you pushed his wrist with your right hand, then your left-hand grabs his wrist from behind the assailant's legs. Be sure to get a good grip and do not let go of his wrist.

Step all the way behind your attacker. Pull his hand through so you can grip his wrist while fully behind him. With your free arm, grab his shirt.

The natural escape is for the attacker to try a

forward roll. With your collar grip, he is unable even to consider rolling away. He is caught.

The final step is critical. If the assailant is standing on the ground with both feet planted firmly on the floor, you do not have complete control of our opponent. Raise the arm, which puts pressure on his testicles, causing him to raise up on his toes.

Now, when he is on his toes, you can walk your attacker to the nearest door. Walk him to the front door through the rooms where everyone can see him and laugh. This causes considerable embarrassment to the attacker. Chances are he will probably leave the party rather than coming back into the front door.

Part Five

Serious Attacks

Chapter 19

Bent Lapel

The whole defense is a double ear slap followed by a leg-sweep throw (Osoto Gari).

This book defines a serious attack as one that can ultimately throw you to the ground, scare you enough to make you compliant, or gain total control over your movements. If someone outright attacks you and the first indication you have of your opponent's intentions is his arms wrapped around you. You must react immediately and hopefully as you have practiced. However, statistically, most danger-ous attacks are preceded with some kind of a hold, like a bear hug, or, as in this move, grabbing your shirt.

Remember, even though you can throw your opponent to the ground and devastate him with kicks and knee drops while he is lying flat on his back, I recom-mend your best course of action is when he is momentarily defense-less, that you flee. Run to safety.

The Attack

The opponent reaches out and grabs your shirt or dress in the upper part of the chest. He does this by pulling you in close to him to startle you, terrify you by his size, and distract you from taking any action. Actually, the attack is usually easy to escape, so do not panic.

First Attack

Take your two hands and keeping your fingers together, cup your hands slightly. Now strike both of the attacker's ears at the same time. The strong slap will drive the air trapped by your hands into his ear. If you hit hard, it a rupture his eardrum and disable him. If not, continue to the throw below.

The Defense

The first step to destroy the other person's balance. You can do this in many ways, but the two easiest methods are listed below. If the opponent has a heavy material shirt, then you grab the outside of his upper arm, about halfway between the elbow and his shoulder. The shirt gives you the best control of his body.

If, however, as in the top picture on the next pages, the attacker has just a flimsy short-sleeved t-shirt, you can not risk that it will stretch and rip. So you must grab either his upper arm or if you can not grip his upper arm firmly, then just below his elbow. In summary, the most ideal grip is first the sleeve of his shirt, then his upper arm, and last his upper forearm.

People sometimes misunderstand the throw. You do not sweep the leg to throw the person. You first put almost all the opponent's weight on that leg, and then you sweep that supporting leg.

You step forward with your left leg as in the picture. Your foot should be equal to or slightly behind his leg. It should not be in front of his toes.

You pull with your left hand down towards your left big toe. This pull shifts the assailant's weight to his right leg. At the same time, your right arm pushes on his left shoulder. You bear down towards his rear, but as if you are moving a titled wheel. You drive back and circularly, around towards your left toe. These two actions load all the weight on the opponent's right foot.

Although not allowed in judo, in the street there are no rules. I have seen this technique taught in the U.S. Army where the right-hand shoots out and with the palm of the hand strike under his chin to throw him off balance. I do not necessarily recommend this alternative move, as it is unnecessary and results in a less violent throw. Nevertheless, the chin strike method will throw the individual.

Now with your right leg step behind your attacker and point your big toe towards the ground. By pointing your toes, it forces you to turn out your hip and shift your weight to your left leg. Remember you are throwing the attacker directly to his weak point. In doing so, you are pulling his shoulder around and down, and his other arm down.

When you sweep with your right foot, slide it about an inch or two off the ground. (When you are advanced and comfortable with the throw it can be done sweeping your foot high up to your waist as you throw. But for your purposes, there is no reason to strive for this degree of perfection and force. It takes too much practice to be so proficient with this technique.

Again, while not part of the throw, when the individual hits the ground, he is usually momentarily stunned, if not hurt. But, if the attacker looks like he could still get up and continue the attack, you can always kick him in the head.

Chapter 20

Straight Lapel

The whole defense is defending someone who holds you with his elbow straight, so his arm is stiff and straight.

In the previous attack, the person grabbed your upper shirt with his arm bent. Here, he grabs you with his arm straight, his elbow stiff and often locked straight.

You reach out and grab his wrist with both hands. The trick of this grip is that you do not raise your shoulders. If there is a movement of your shoulders, the opponent will sense something is happening and might react.

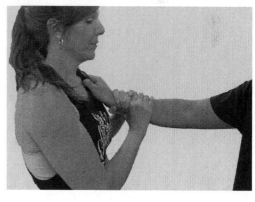

Instead, raise your hands up your cheek keeping them close to your body. Now grab his wrists, with both knuckles facing up to the ceiling.

Now to do two things simultaneously. With your left foot step forward parallel to your other foot. You are now facing at a 90-degree angle to where you were. This shift in location twists his wrist. At the same time, you turn his wrist towards your mid-line, rotating his elbow facing upward toward the sky. Your left elbow is bent but putting pressure directly on his elbow joint. By forcing down, you drive him downward.

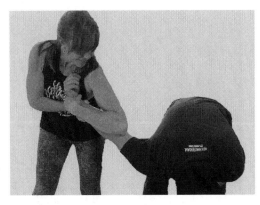

From this dominant position, you can use your right hand to do a "judo chop" to the back of his neck. Or you can easily kick with your right foot, connecting solidly with his face.

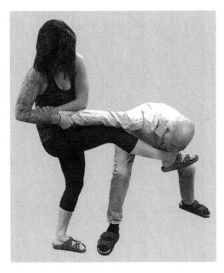

Chapter 21

Arm Across Shoulders

In this defense, you give him a rear elbow in the face, followed by a strike in the groin.

In this defense, you are sitting on a park bench outside, or in a chair inside, and an opponent sits down beside you and puts his arm across your shoulders. Usually, he does so with his "heavy hand," meaning he puts considerable weight on your shoulders, show you how strong and in control he is.

You immediately lean towards him and drive your elbow back into his face. Some people like bracing their elbow with the other hand because they do not think they will generate enough power otherwise. Personally, I do

not like the two hand approach. You can strike much faster with just one elbow. The speed on a one-handed strike with your whole body generates substantial power. You need to strike with full force if you are doing a one-armed blow.

Your elbow is a powerful, strong weapon. Aim for his nose or anywhere around there with the point of your elbow or the flat of your elbow. If you don't feel the first strike did enough damage, you can always quickly follow up with a second rear elbow strike.

Next, strike his face with your other hand. You stand up quickly and face your opponent sitting on the bench. You can punch, chop, or heal-hand him.

There is a difference of opinion among instructors. I happen not to like advising students to punch the attacker in the head with a straight punch. Striking straight on to his head can be like striking a wall; the face bone can be as hard as a rock if hit certain ways. I feel why take the risk of a head or chin strike when you can damage him so many other ways.

You can punch with a hook to the side of the face, strike with the palm of your hand to his chin or nose, or drive your fingers in his eyes.

Standing Up

This also works if you are standing up and your aggressor puts his arm across your shoulder. The only difference is sometimes the second strike is more accessible to the groin than the face.

Chapter 22

Arm Across Shoulders

In this defense, you strike his groin, followed by a strike to the eyes.

This is an alternate defense when you are sitting on a park bench outside, or in a chair inside, and an attacker sits down beside you and puts his arm across your shoulders.

Before you slide right into your attack, you might first see if just getting up and moving to another chair is an option. Sometimes just removing yourself from the situating might be sufficient. However, assuming moving, screaming out loud that this man next to you is attacking you, or other such techniques are ineffective, then you must resort to a martial arts escape.

The first move is a strike to the groin. However, because you are sitting down, you must take extra effort to generate the full power of the blow's potential. You do this by bringing your hand up by your ear, to maximize the total striking distance. See the photo on the right. Note that you also turn your body slightly, so that when you do attack, you will have the twisting of your body to add to the natural swing of your strike.

Using the knife edge of your hand, strike down between the opponent's legs to drive the chop into his groin.

Now switch to your other arm, the one farthest away from your attacker. Bring it up in preparation to strike.

Now strike your attacker in the eyes with a claw hand if you fear for your life.

Alternatively, if you want a less damaging move, use the heal of your hand and strike him under the chin.

Standing Up

This also works if you are standing up and your aggressor puts his arm across your shoulder.

Chapter 23

Rear Hug Behind Bench
(*Arms Are Free*)

In this defense, you grab the little finger and pull back hard, then follow up with an elbow strike to the face.

Here you are sitting on a park bench in the park or in a chair inside of somewhere, and an attacker sneaks up behind you. He stays behind the wooden bench or the chair and reaches over to grab you around the chest, but under the arms. Thus, your arms are free to move about.

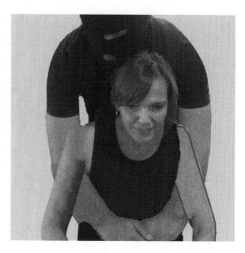

In this picture, because the bench is somewhat low, you cannot see the back of the wooden seat. Actually, it does not matter much if the back side is high or low.

The first thing you do since your arms are free is to grasp the little finger of the arm that is on top. That little finger should be easy

enough to grab. Just stick your
fingers between and grab, then
pull the little finger as hard as
you can towards your elbow
and upward in the air. You are
trying to break his finger and
to loosen the attacker's grip
around your waist.

If you cannot get the little finger, then make a fist and using
the first joint of your fingers,
rub them as hard and as briskly as you an across his knuckles. That
action should cause his hands to separate.

Now with a rear elbow strike
him in the face. If his head
is low than yours, you can
remain seating. If the opponent's head is higher, you
might have to rise from the
bench a little.

If he is still standing, strike
him again with the elbow.
That would be two quick, suc-
cessive strikes.

Chapter 24

Rear Bear Hug
Behind Bench
(*Arms Not Free*)

In this defense, you reach around behind you with both arms and grab his head. You then throw him over your shoulder onto the ground.

While sitting on a park bench or in a chair somewhere, the attacker walks up behind the seat or chair. He reaches over and grabs you over your arms.

Because the back of the bench is between you and the attacker, he is unable to grab you tightly as he would for a bear hug if you were standing up.

With both hands reach up behind you and wrap your hands together around his neck. Because he is so close to you, this position is easy to obtain.

Now that he is sealed close to you, his center of balance has changed from his belly button to your shoulder. His center of mass is over your shoulder, so you just need to lean forward and put your head between your knees. Your opponent is automatically loaded on your back and

carried forward. He flips over your back to land heavy on the ground before your feet.

If he is still "feisty," which is somewhat unlikely, just aim a few hard kicks at his head. Now run for safety.

Chapter 25

Rear Hug, Arms Free

(Standing Up)

In this defense, you reach down and pull his foot out from under him and then kick him in the groin.

This is a common attack, especially if the person jumps out of the bushes and grips you under the arms and from your rear. He usually squeezes your stomach a little and yells in your ear to be good, and he will not hurt you. It is also a relatively straightforward situation from which to escape.

The first thing you do is to squat down so that your feet are in a wide stance. If your feet are too close together, you will have a hard time reaching between your legs.

Now bend down and reach between your legs and grab his leg near the ankle. It is easier to grasp near the ankle because the leg is not as thick and muscular. If you have a hard time reaching his ankles, it means you did not spread your feet wide enough apart.

The next step is to pull the leg up to your crotch. This action alone will not throw him. Instead, as you pull the leg up, you *squat lower,* so you put pressure forcing his leg and therefore his balance lower and lower. You are pressing at or near to his kneecap. You continue pulling until he is thrown back to the ground.

If he does not fall backward, you probably have not squatted low enough to destroy his balance.

Your attacker is now lying on the ground. Do not release his foot. This is not a violent fall, and if he has access to both feet, he can roll away and try to get up. So keep a tight hold on his foot. Also, note in the picture that woman's stance if relatively straight up and she is looking around to make sure no friends are nearby.

Now, while keeping a firm grip on his ankle, shift all your weight to your other foot. You do not swing your foot into a kick. Instead, you raise your knee up to waist high with your foot hanging parallel to the floor. Now turn your hip slightly so you can see where you are striking, and drive your heal back into his crotch.

If he still looks "feisty," quickly shoot him a second kick, but much harder, to the crotch. Your kick or kicks should leave him floundering on the ground and unable to run after you. Just walk away quickly.

Chapter 26

Rear Hug, Arms Free

(Standing Up)

In this defense, you drive a rear elbow into his face and then strike the groin with the knife edge of your hand.

This defense is an alternative form of response when the attacker grabs you from behind, under the arms.

In this attack, the opponent aims to immobilize and control you and your movements. It is an intimidation technique that works on most untrained women. Conversely, when a man applies this technique against another man, he is trying to squeeze the ribs to crack them and cause maximum damage. In that situation, this same strategy may work, but you must apply the moves faster than in the mere immobilization attack.

The first part of the defense is to swivel your hips to the side so that you have a clean shot at his groin. Since his grip is above your waist, there is no difficulty in moving your hips. Then swing your arm down hard with the edge of your hand ("judo chop") striking hard into the opponent's groin.

Then using the same hand, twist your upper body mildly, and strike him in the face with your elbow.

If after these two attacks he is still standing, repeat the elbow strikes repeatedly and rapidly until he drops or withdraws. Now you can escape and run to safety.

Chapter 27

Front Hug, Arms Free

*In this defense, you grab his chin and his head
or hair in both hands and twist, throwing
him to the ground.*

In this attack the opponent walks up to you, perhaps asking a question, and when he is close to you suddenly grabs you under the arms. He then pulls you in close to him, threatening you if you do not cooperate.

The first step is to place one hand on the back of his head and the other under his chin. Both hands must be pressed firmly against his head. Some schools teach grabbing the hair instead of the back of the head, and if your attacker has hair, you can use the alternate grip, if you prefer.

Now twist his head side-wards, destroying his balance. Continue pulling in a circular motion, but pull his head towards your hips. He will drop like a rock to the ground.

Be careful in twisting his neck to do so in a smooth, gently twist. A hard jerk and twist could break his neck, resulting in paralysis or even death.

Of course, once on the ground, you can kick and stomp him until you feel he is unable to run after you when you escape.

Chapter 28

Front Hug, Arms Free

*In this defense, you strike his ears then follow
up with a knee kick to the groin.*

This is an alternate defense to
when the opponent walks up to
you and grabs you under the arms.
Your arms are free, but he holds
you around your waist, and he is
facing you.

The first thing you do is cup your
hands slightly. Then slap them
forcefully and simultaneously
against both of his ears. This
attack may well rupture his ear-
drums.

Now push your opponent back, by using your hands against his shoulders. You need the distance, so you don't smother your kick. If you do not have sufficient distance between you, then you cannot really deliver a powerful kick.

As you step back, go to a forward stance, one foot considerably ahead of the other. Remember you want to be about 90-degrees to the strong point, the line between his ankles. Now drive your knee into his groin. Note how he is being pulled closer by the hands on his shoulders.

Chapter 29

Front Choke

*In this defense, you strike the back of his neck
and then deliver uppercut punch to his ribs.*

Here the attacker chokes you with his arm approximately straight, usually with the intent to make it hard for you to breath, hoping to scare you so much you will do whatever he says.

The front choke is one of those moves, like the wrist escapes of chapter eight, where the thumbs provide an easy release. Look at a front choke, when the man is standing in front of you with his hands around your neck choking you. As he squeezes, you can't walk forward or stand still.

But, his thumbs are on the front of your neck, and just his fingertips are holding you at the back of the neck. All you need to do is step back or twist backward and sideways, and he can not hold on to you.

In this technique, you are facing him as your opponent faces you. You step back, so your strong side faces his weak side at a 90-degree angle. This back twisting action causes him to release your neck.

As you step back, reach out and grab his arm. Now pull that arm towards the floor. Do not redirect the angle of the pull. Instead, just pull towards his foot. His balance is destroyed, and your arm controls his movement.

As your opponent is in that bent position, the back of his neck is exposed. Use your arm and strike the upper part of his neck. To generate the full speed and power you need, make a long circular swing of your arm.

Now you strike his ribs with upper-cut punches three times. Note how the punches are hitting the front side of the ribs. If you strike the curved sides of the bones, they are strong at the curvature.

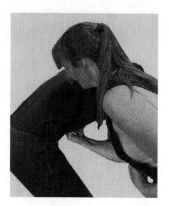

Second, you strike high, so you are hitting the two lower floating ribs. The floating ribs are not connected to the breastbone, so they have less support and are easier to break.

If your uppercut punches did not break a rib or disable him, then use your right foot and kick into the side of his knee joint, driving it directly into the ground. Now pull on his rear collar in a 45-degree angle to the ground, slamming his head into the ground. You should be able to walk away safely now.

Chapter 30

Front Bear Hug
(Arms Locked Up)

*In this defense, you strike the back of his neck
and then deliver uppercut punch to his ribs.*

This is an alternate defense to when the opponent walks up to you and grabs you over the arms. Your arms are not free, he holds you around your waist, and he is facing you.

The fact that he holds you over your arms seems at first glance as if he has you wrapped up in an immovable situation. In fact, many techniques will release you from this situation.

The first part of the escape is to drive your two thumbs into his groin. You take your two thumbs and aim for his penis. It may sound obnoxious, but it is a very effective move. Your opponent will back up, as he is doing in the picture.

I have found women have a hard time practicing this part of the escape. If you cannot practice this move in the studio or in your own practice, how are you going to do it in the street? You must make yourself do this part of the move correctly. He will move so you will not be hurting your training partner.

Now, grab his waist with both hands. He is still leaning on you, so your balance is somewhat compromised, and holding on to your attacker gives you more support.

Your opponent is already far enough away so you will not smother your kick. Bring your knee up sharply into his groin.

If for some reason you did not hit him securely in his groin, strike a second time with another knee to the groin.

After the knee, he should drop his hands on you. Now hit with your elbow across his chin. Do not hit his chin straight on, but hit the side of his cheek and spin his head.

If he has not dropped to the ground, spin your hips and throw the other elbow to the side of his chin. Keep striking until he falls, although usually, he drops after the kick to the groin.

Chapter 31

Obnoxious Hook-Up in Car

You can be in a car in a romantic position enjoying yourself when your "hook-up" suddenly decides he wants what you do not. You need to stop him and to let that person know you are no longer enjoying the intimacy. He needs to see that you will fight to retain your dignity and the right to control your own body.

Fighting inside a car is always difficult. If you are in the driver's seat, the steering wheel obstructs many of your potential moves, and the seat belt further restricts your movements. If you are in the back seat on your back with your hook-up on top, you are fighting from a severely defensive position. If you are sitting up kissing, much depends on which arm is free and where you are seated in the car. There are so many variations that pictures cannot cover all the scenarios. Instead, broad generalization will be helpful.

Remember the rhyme from chapter six: "Eyes and ears, then down the middle, throat, solar plexus, and groin. Then the hands and feet." These targets are very vulnerable in a car. You can ram your fingers into his eyes, strike the ears. There are no rules. If you have the option, you can even bite the ear off. You do whatever it takes to avoid being raped.

The elbow is a very effective close in weapon, strong and powerful.

Use it to distract your attacker, then go for his groin. The groin is the easy target that leaves most men momentarily helpless.

The fingers are good for attacks. Just grab two fingers and pull them as far apart as possible. Or, grasp only one finger and pull it in ways that finger was not designed to go. The fingers are very painful.

If he puts his hand around you, it is like a bear hug in some ways. You can snap your head forward hitting him in the nose, and do so repeatedly until he lets you free. Or, if he has your arms tightly pinned, try hitting his groin, multiple time until he releases you. I had one student who told me she grabbed her now ex-boyfriend's penis and twisted it as far as it would go. She then pushed him out the door and left him lying on the curb.

If possible, you can maneuver your back against a door, with your feet facing your opponent. Now you can kick him. Maybe even force him out of the car. You can then lock the doors and drive away. If your attacker has hair, grabbing a handful will cause his head to follow in the direction you pull him.

The rhyme listing the vital points on the body states only a few of the most used strike points on an attacker. There are many others. Your attacker's skin under his upper arm, between the armpit and the elbow, is sensitive. Pinch it as hard as you can and twist at the same time will cause considerable pain, and allow you to attack a primary target, the groin.

If you are located in a shopping center, sometimes just pressing on the horn and keep pushing it will make enough noise to scare the guy into leaving. Or, lower the window and yell to a passerby, "Help he is trying to rape me. Call the police." These may not be effective, but they might be worth trying.

Look at your situation and gauge your reaction accordingly. Do not give in if there is still room and ability to fight. Do not be afraid to leave your vehicle and run for help, if appropriate. Hopefully, if you escape from the car, try to take the keys with you.

Author's Advice

The following is my own opinion, but it is based on many years of teaching women and listening to their discussions about techniques that appear in this book. Almost all women have no problem reacting quickly and without remorse when attacked by a stranger. They will use their training without hesitation even though many of the techniques can be quite devastating. However, these very same women verbally express doubt about attacking a boyfriend or a known person who goes too far in a car, at a party, or in a bedroom.

Remember that over half of all rapes are committed by someone you already know. Assuming you are kissing someone and suddenly he decides to take your hugs and kisses to an entirely different level. You tell him "no" in a firm voice, and he ignores you. You raise your arms and push his shoulders away, again telling him "no." I call this the "tipping point."

At this tipping point, stage, too many women tell me they are reluctant to defend themselves, feeling it is not severe enough to warrant a counter attack. They still think they have control of the situation. So, they wait until their suddenly aggressive "hook up" for the night is on top of them.

Now the situation cries for drastic action, and unfortunately, when it goes this far, it usually takes far more punishing action to stop your attacker. A mere slap in the face is not enough. Now you need to consider action like ears, throat, groin, hands, and feet. Further, you will probably need to strike your attacker enough to hurt him before he will stop and let you up.

The time to act is the at the tipping point. Then, a sharp slap to the face or thumb jab into the throat will usually stop your date. When your line is crossed, do not be reluctant to act, because you may have to react harder, stronger and more aggressively than would have been needed earlier.

Part Six

Fighting from the Ground

Chapter 32

You on Ground and He Standing Up

Using kicks and a leg throw to defend your-self while lying on the ground while your attacker is standing over you.

There is an old, often cited adage that says in a fight you should never go to the ground. For a woman, especially, that is good advice. On the floor, you are more likely to be fighting strength against strength.

Even the mixed martial arts ("MMA") advises staying off the ground in a street fight if all you are using is "tournament" techniques. As Rener Gracie, head instructor of the entire Gracie Ju-Jitsu Academy, said in a well-publicized video posted on the Internet: the man on the bottom is taught to keep his hands in close to guard his neck against chokes and his arms in tight from armlocks. Do that in the street as the man on top can rain down punches and elbow strikes while you are in a somewhat defenseless position.

In a real fight, you should be pushing your opponent away, so you get back to your feet and control the distance. Tournament fighting is significantly different from street fighting ju-jitsu.

As a woman, unless you are a skilled MMA street-fighter, avoid the ground. That does not mean you will always have that choice. But, if you do find yourself on the ground, you are far from defenseless. Your primary goal is to avoid being hurt while getting to your feet as fast as possible. This chapter talks about not getting hurt while on the ground.

This technique has three significant advantages going for you.

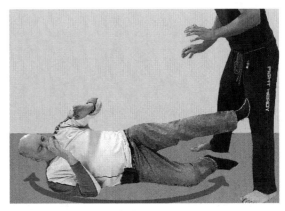

<u>In Defensive Position</u>. First, you are not flat on your back. Instead, you are basically on your side, with your bottom knee bent. Your lower arm is bent with your elbow on the floor, and your hand is blocking your face from any attack. The upper arm is also protecting your body and preventing him from getting down on his knees and wrestling with you on the ground. Your feet are facing your attacker. It is hard for him to find an opening to hurt you.

<u>Rotate to Keep Feet Towards Him</u>. Second, by having your knee and shoulder on the ground, with your arm also on the floor, you can quickly rotate your body. Keep your feet facing your attacker, and as he moves around, you keep moving to keep your feet facing him. If he moves to the left, you move to the left, so he is always facing your feet.

<u>You Can Kick Him</u>. Third, you have the defense of your upper leg. It stays bent and near your other knee, but it immediately strikes out with a powerful kick if the attacker gets in range. In the above picture, I am kicking his leg as he gets too close. The kick can do

damage, prevents him from getting close, and may drive him back enough for you to get up. You may need to do 15 or 20 kicks before he gives up and goes away, or before you have driven him far enough back that you can get up. (The net chapter discussing getting to your feet.)

If you are careful, you can even get one foot behind his heal, and the other foot kicks his upper thigh. The two actions work like scissors. One foot pulls the heal in close to your body, the upper foot pushes the upper leg away from you.

The scissors action will throw your opponent to the ground. This has two effects. First, it gives you time to get to your feet. Second, it reverses the position and places him on the ground.

If you can execute the foot throw, you can escape. However, since the throw is effective but not violent, you may feel the need to kick him in the head a few times before fleeing.

Chapter 33

Getting to Your Feet

A technique for safely getting to your feet when lying on the ground.

There are several methods of getting to your feet once you have been on the ground. By kicking from the floor, described in the last chapter, you can drive the attacker back out of kicking range. Then you can seek to raise up to standing. The method shown here is one of the easiest procedures to get to your feet.

Once you have distracted or distanced the attacked a few feet back from you by kicks, it is time to get up. You can only do so when you think it is safe to do so. Do not risk getting up unless you feel there is sufficient time to do so safely. It should not take you more than 60 to 90 seconds.

While you are on the ground and have established a "safe area," being the distance of your

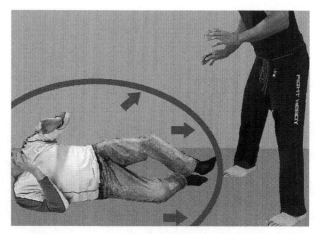

kicking range. When you get up, you do not want to cross that imaginary line and encroach into "his" territory. If you extend into his area, it becomes easier for him to strike you as you are standing up.

If you do not cross that imaginary line, he is likely to see it as a threat, less likely to pass into your area, and less likely to realize how quickly you are up off the ground. Then, if he does come after you, fortunately, you still have your hands and feet for protection.

Do not get up until it is safe, and do not stop kicking until he backs off. Some attackers will get frustrated and leaving quickly, others seem to think it is a game that you will give up after a while. As long as you maintain your willingness to strike, you are in a good position.

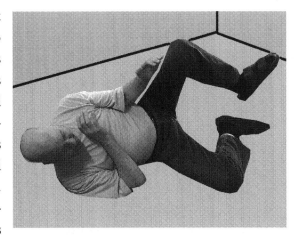

The Technique

For simplicity the leg closest to the sky will be called the "upper leg," and the other leg referred to as the "lower leg."

The first step in raising to your feet is putting the foot of your upper leg down on the ground. Then

rise about six to twelve inches from the ground, supporting yourself on your elbow and your upper leg's foot. Extend your other leg out straight.

This next part, while not hard, is the only skillful part of the technique. You bring your lower leg back under your arm. It is in front of you, and you swing it to the back under your arm, so your leg is behind you. This is the secret of this technique's success.

As you stand up, your bent upper leg becomes your front foot. Because your foot is located in your "safe territory," you are not going forward into "his" area.

Now just stand up. Although hard to see in this picture, because it is emphasizing foot placement, you should continuously be looking at your attacker and watching his movements.

As you entirely come to stand up, assume whatever type of stance you are comfortable fighting from. This stance was chosen because once the opponent realizes you are on your feet, he often rushes forward to try to stop you. A front snap kick is one of the easiest ways to prevent him from coming at you. You are now free to run or fight, as the situation allows.

Chapter 334

Sitting on Chest

The attacker sits on your chest, pinning your arms as a means of total control.

I am always amazed when I show this attack to women, and they look at me with that uncertain look, asking why in the world would anyone in the human race ever get in that position.

For men, it started when they were boys in school. This was the ultimate "win" position in a school fight. The opponent sat on your chest pinning your arms and could hit you at will whenever he wanted. Men who had no ju-jitsu, wrestling, or karate training still remember this move and such men think it dominates and gives them complete control.

What is surprising to most men is that when they sit on your chest, their center of balance is over the center of your chest. By analogy, it is like building a tall apartment building over a water mattress. It is not a stable ground. So, too with this attack.

You need only bridge and twist to one side to throw your opponent off. Since his center of balance is actually on *you*, as you move, so moves his once solid center of balance.

First, make a fist with one of your hands under his knee. At the same time, bring up the leg on that same side and plant your foot flat on the ground.

Next, you bridge upward using the power of your flat foot and leg power, which throws his balance even more forward. Then, still in one move, throw a hook punch all the way to your opposite side, keeping it about 6 inches off the floor.

As you throw the punch, roll your shoulder over and your upper leg over so you are more than at a 90-degree angle. You have effectively rolled over to almost a 45-degree angle to the floor.

If the attacker is not thrown off, you did not roll all the way over. A gentle roll or a roll for only half a circle will not throw the attacker off. As this is not a violent throw, you immediately follow up which either a strike to the groin, or if you end up higher to his head, then an eye gouge.

Chapter 35

In Rape-Choke Position

The attacker is in the rape position, with one hand holding you to the ground by choking you and the other hand reaching to undo his pants.

You can assume the man wants to rape you from the front (which according to one well respected statistical source is how over 96 percent of rapes occur).

The attacker is going to have to be between your legs groin-to-groin.

To keep you from escaping, he usually "straight-arms" you with one hand choking you, while the other hand is generally fumbling to unzip his pants.

(If he has two hands on your shoulders holding you down, another common rape position, you do a different type of technique discussed in a later chapter.)

The first thing you should do if possible is to put your knee up across your body. It is not part of this move, but if you can do it, and often you can, it prevents the attacker from getting too close. It gives you a degree of control. However, the knee block is not a requirement of breaking out of this attack.

Assume he is choking you with his left hand; meaning he is probably right-handed and using his other hand to drop his pants.

Take your left arm and reach over his arm and towards your right. Now, bend your elbow, reverse your movement, and slam your elbow into his left elbow. Three things should happen. First, it should collapse his straight arm, so his left arm is bent. Second, the bent arm will

throw him closer to you. Third, it will throw more of his weight up and forward, making it much harder to pull down his pants.

Now, the next step is to throw him off of you. You take your left hand

and place it behind and on top of his head. You take your right arm and bring it up under this chin. With your plan make a tight grip on his chin. Because he is now closer to you, it should be easy to reach his head and secure your hold.

Now twist his head in a counter-clockwise rotation. He will have to follow his head or risk breaking his neck. In practice and probably in an attack situation you would want to roll your hips to the left helping throw him off you. This twisting means your body helps him turn, keeps him from risking breaking his neck.

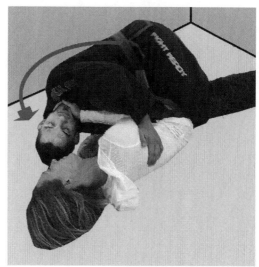

It is essential to practice this move many times, so you commit to memory the roll over your hips, so he doesn't break his neck. Without you turning and rolling your body, you risk breaking his neck!

If after the above technique, he still looks aggressive, you can claw the eyes, strike the ear with the palm of your hand, or take your hand on his chin and squeeze his Adam's Apple hard. Then you can escape, and he should not follow.

Chapter 36

In Rape-Choke Position

Again, the attacker is in the rape position, with one hand holding you to the ground by choking you.

This technique is called a triangle strangle, and although it is more advanced, many women with strong legs seem to like it. For that reason, I am including the choke as an escape. However, note that it takes more skill and all the aspects of this choke must be properly applied to work.

Basically what you are doing is putting his head in a squeeze and cutting off blood to the brain. It should render him unconscious for a short time. When the attacker goes unconscious, release him, and you do not want to deliberatively deprive his brain of oxygen for too long a period of time and cause permanent brain damage or death.

In ju-jitsu, there is a difference between a choke and a strangle. A choke is a Western concept of cutting off the person's breath by squeezing his windpipe or neck. Conversely, a strangle is an Eastern concept of cutting off the flow of blood to the brain by pressing shut the carotid artery or arteries on the side of the neck.

For simplicity, assume the attacker is right-handed and is chocking or holding you down with his right hand. His right hand will be called the "trapped arm," and his other arm will be the "free arm." The method below is one of several procedures to apply this technique.

The first step is to put your left foot flat against his right hip, to pre-

vent him from getting closer. At the same time your left-hand grabs his trapped wrist so he cannot remove it. Simultaneously, you push his free arm down between your legs so it won't get caught up in the triangular strangle.

Now, using your left foot on his hip as your fulcrum, raise your hip way up off the ground, 6 to 12 inches if possible. At the same time raise your right leg skyward.

Now, stop bridging and bring your hips back to the ground. As you

do so, bring your knee down on the back of his neck. His neck must be close to your knee, as your knee will be pressing on his carotid artery during the strangling part of this technique.

Next quickly raise your left leg that was on his hip upward and bend the knee to lock

your right ankle into the crook of
your left knee. You want your leg
over his neck to be near the knee
in your upraised leg.

You grip two hands on the wrist of
his choking arm and pull it across
your body. Ordinarily, it would be
hard to move his arm, but at the time you pull the arm, you also
bridge high with your hips once again. Now the arm moves easily.

You have to pull it
under his chin so
his hand will be
able to squeeze
his carotid artery
on the side of his
neck.

If his arm is over
his chin, you will
not be able to
squeeze enough
actually to strangle him. At the same time, as you pull his arm across
your body, fully bend your leg in the arm, so your knee clamps your
other ankle. This creates a triangle-like shape around his head.

At the same time, when your hips are again on the ground from
bridging, pull your hips towards his trapped hand. So you are turning your hips slightly sideways to him. This will create more pressure
on his head. This is especially important if you shorter legs. It places
more pressure from the legs around the neck.

Now, squeeze your knees together, and with two hands pull his head down into your chest. Controlling his head adds more pressure to the choke, and also helps you control his body so he cannot easily stand up.

Keep up this pressure until 15 seconds or more after he goes limp and uncon- scious. Then roll away and quickly escape. This is a technique that requires practice to perfect, but  once mastered, is an effective technique.

If you are having difficulty doing this art, it is because this move is more advanced. In such case, instead of getting frustrated with this technique, focus on other escapes. The method of the previous chapter will free you from this attack with little effort.

Chapter 37

In Rape Position

The attacker is in the rape position, both of his knees between your legs. Here he is not holding you down with one hand choking you but is holding you with both arms.

In this technique, your attacker is between your leg, his hips to your hips. This is the other most popular rape position. Here he threatens you while holding both your shoulders to the ground. He thinks he has full control over you while you are under threat and on your back.

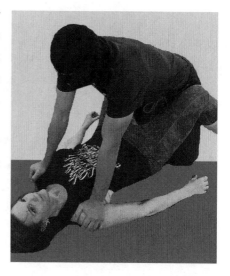

The first step is to place your feet up on his shoulders. If possible, try to place them in a gentle scissors action around his head, meaning your ankles are crossed behind his head. If you cannot scissors his neck, the technique will still work, but it just takes a little more pressure.

If you do scissor him, do not put much pressure on his neck. It does not help the technique, and it will only wear you out. Basically, your scissors are pulling him forward off balance.

At the same time reach up with both arms and grab his hands. Now raise your hips up towards the ceiling. Note in the picture how my butt is about six inches off the ground.

It may seem odd, but you want to keep your hips as close to your attacker as possible as you raise them up. When the hips are close and up, it is hard for the attacker to undo his clothes or take yours off. With your hips raised, it is much harder for your attacker to achieve penetration.

As you raise your hips, spread his arms wide while squeezing your knees together. This combined effect of your knees pushing his elbows inward and pulling his arms outward puts the attacker in a painful arm lock. Pull the arms far enough, and you can break his elbows. Or, release your head scissors and kick the attacker in the face while holding his arms. Remember, your goal is to disorient him just enough so you can escape.

Part VII

Other Attacks

Chapter 38

Headlocks

There are three attacks that men commonly use against other men when they are wrestling or controlling another person. It is not commonly used against a woman, yet a woman cannot afford to be totally unprepared for any of these attacks. Statistics show that they are occasionally used. The first is the headlock (discussed in this chapter), and the other two are presented in the next two chapters. For some situations, several methods are shown as you must be ready for some variations in the attacker and the attack.

Using Hair Grip

The Attack

Your attacker grabs you around the head (or sometimes just the neck) and cranks your head to his side, so you are bent over. The attacker then applies pressure on your head or neck if you don't do what he wants.

Grab His Hair

With the hand that is closest to him (your inside arm) and grab a large handful of hair. Assuming he has enough hair, grab from the top of his head, not the rear. The reason is the top allows you to crank his neck more and throw him farther off balance than a rear hair grip.

Throw to Ground

Pull his hair, so his head is face up towards the sky, throwing him off balance to his rear. Now, step backward with your rear foot to keep your balance. As you do so, pull his head towards the ground. Surprisingly, this is a rather violent throw, but for any reason, your attacker still looks active, you can kick him several times before your escape.

Using Nose Lever

Use the Nose

If he has short hair, which is not uncommon, there is not enough hair to grab. Instead just bring your hand over his head and down by his nose. Put the edge of your hand (the so-called "judo chop" part) under his nose. Now throw him using the same means as above, only with his nose. This is actually a more violent fall than just pulling his hair.

Strike to Groin

Groin Strike

Some men will either have you so far for-ward that it is hard to bring your arm up by his hair, or they have short hair and turn their nose so you can't get it. It doesn't hap-pen often, but it is not unheard of. In this case, step forward with your outside feet towards the middle of his two feet. As you do so, bend a little lower so there will be no resistance, and with a strong uppercut, strike his groin.

Chapter 39

Hammerlocks

A hammerlock is a common wrestling hold where you force someone's arm up behind their back and towards their head. It is painful, and if applied to the maximum can probably injure the shoulder joint. Because it is so painful, the hammerlock is often used to control someone.

The Attack

Since 90% of the United States population is right-handed, assume it is your right arm is one trapped and twisted behind your back.

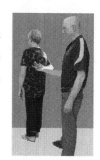

Unwind the Twist

Just as you can untie a knot, you can unwind the hammerlock. You have to bend your back down low (without bending your legs) and step with your left foot in front.

Side Kick to Knee

After you have stepped out, bring your right leg up and do a side-kick into his knee. If he does not drop your hand, keep repeating the sidekick until he collapses or releases your hand.

Chapter 40

Full Nelson

Usually, a full nelson is an attack used by one man against another man, but occasionally it seeps over as an attack against a woman.

The technique shown below uses three levels of defenses. The easiest is the foot stomp, and if that does not release you, then immediately apply the side knee kick. If you still have not escaped, then and only then, you follow up with the groin strike-to-leg pull.

I am against hip throws and also leg-to-ground takedowns because they require far more skill than the karate techniques below. Unless you are skilled in hip throws, some opponents can block you if try a hip throw and are not competent in that technique. As for leg-to-ground takedowns, I dislike a woman voluntarily going to the ground, where your opponent is probably stronger and faster. There are other defensive techniques still available and easier to use.

The Attack

 A full nelson is a wrestling hold applied when your opponent is behind you. He passes his arms under your armpits and then places both palms against your neck. From there he applies pressure against your neck, either to cause you pain or to force you to the ground. With your arms locked you cannot reach behind you to grab his head or body. It is a harder holder to break than some others, but it can be broken quite effectively.

First Level

Block Neck Pressure

Immediately put both of your hands on your forehead. Put the back of your palms against your forehead, and push your head upward. The angle of your arms against his wrists stops some pressure, and both hands against your head should stop the down-ward pressure and allow you time to counter-attack.

Shin-to-Instep Stomp

Slam the heal of your dominate foot into his shin, about halfway between your attacker's knee and his ankle. Then stomp straight down along the shinbone and into his instep with the heel of the foot. There is a nerve that runs across the top of the ankle bone, and stopping on it causes considerable pain. Theoreti-cally, if you stomped hard enough, you could damage and even break the ankle bone.

Second Level

Kick to Inside Knee

If the above shin-bone, ankle stomp did not release you, then immediately move to the level two technique. At the same time, be sure to keep your hand on your forehead.

Drive the heal portion of the flat of your foot into the *side* of his knee, buckling it inward. The biggest mistake beginners make is trying to kick the front of the kneecap. It is far more damaging to kick the side of the knee. If one kick doesn't work, kick it a second time.

Third Level

Step to Side

Assuming you are right-handed, step with your right foot about 12 to 18 inches to the side. At the same time, lower your hips, which will make it even harder for your attacker to put pressure on your neck. It also sets you up for the next part of your move.

Groin Strike

Bend way forward at the waist, and with your left hand strike your attacker's groin. Use the knife edge of your hand (the so-called "judo chop") and swing it to the rear into his crotch. If he doesn't cry out in pain, strike a second time only harder.

Leg Lift

Squat down low on your knees, reach between your legs, and grab his ankle. Pull his foot forward between your legs throw-

ing him to the ground. If he doesn't fall, it is because you did not remain squatting low and deep. It is the low squat that is most responsible for the throw.

Kick to Groin

Drive the heal of your foot backward in a stomp-type kick into his groin. Be sure to look at his groin, so your balance will automatically shift to your other foot. This way, when you kick you should retain your upright balance.

Chapter 41

Rear Knife
and Choke Defense

This book has purposely avoided discussion of fending off an armed attack. First, statistically, they are only a minority of weapon attacks on women. Secondly, weapon defense is an advanced course requiring a full book and months of practice. However, since one of the students in my school encountered an attempted rape by a man holding a knife from behind to her throat, it is worth discussing this one move.

Here the attacker approaches you from behind and puts one arm (usually his left arm) around your neck, and his dominant hand (here his right arm) holds a knife up so, you see it pointed at your throat. He then tells you something like, "don't make any noise and do as I say and you will come out alive."

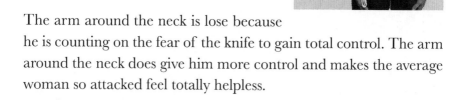

The arm around the neck is lose because he is counting on the fear of the knife to gain total control. The arm around the neck does give him more control and makes the average woman so attacked feel totally helpless.

The first step is to bring both hands up to your shoulder area. The trick is to keep your shoulders rock solid and unmoving, so you are not telegraphing that you are moving your arms. Also, as you sneak your arms up to your body, keep them close to your skin so they cannot be seen.

Your left arm reaches across your body, and you lay your forearm under his knife arm. Your right arm goes behind his knife arm. You completely ignore the arm around your neck. You also just start to turn your body to the side.

Side View

Now, pivot in your left foot 180 degrees. In other words, you were facing his front, and after the pivot, you are facing your attacker's rear. As you do so, your left arm grabs your right arm. As you do so, you will be cranking his shoulder into an unnatural position, from which he has no strength in which to move. (See the picture on the next page.)

Now, pull your arms strongly towards the ground, slamming him into the cement or grass. Since he chose to use a weapon and potentially risk your life, you can't afford to be kind. Kick him several times in the head as hard as you can. This should cause a brain concussion making him incapable of following you as you run away.

Part Eight

High Risk Occupations

Chapter 42

College Freshman

You may think you are ready for college, but you may not be as prepared as you might think. Some may believe this chapter should have been toned down to be less uncomfortable to high school seniors and college students, but the nature of self-defense is that you must have some comprehension of the real risks before you can consider protecting yourself. The most significant risk is rape! The statistics vary, especially on the definition of sexual assault, and between colleges and universities, but four statistics appear in most nationwide studies:

- During the freshman year, it is estimated that 15% of women students are raped (although less than 5% are reported to police). That means of every ten freshman women in colleges and universities, more than one was raped during their freshman year. Your odds are quite high that YOU MAY BE RAPED if you do not take necessary precautions.

- For college women, the most dangerous part of their life is during the first six weeks of college. The President's Commission on College Violence labels this period as the "redzone." It is the time between orientation and Thanksgiving break.

- 90% of the freshman women who were raped, were raped while incapacitated due to such heavy drinking or drugs to where they were considered incapable of giving consent. The statistics did not differentiate between heavy drinking, extensive drug intake, and date-rape drugs like GHB. Only 10% (the remaining percentage of sexual assaults) were raped by mere physical force.

- In 90% of the rape and attempted rape cases, the woman victim knew their attacker. Many of these attacks were during a date.

Lack Experience to Know the Dangers

These statistics are incredible, and I am sure if they ever took a sizable nationwide study, experts would find most high school seniors and college students are *unaware* of the extreme risk they face. Statistically, you don't have the experience to know when you are in danger. The numbers are far too large to ignore. You cannot blindly assume it won't happen to you.

- One large study of over 150,000 women at 27 major universities found that <u>one in four</u> women were sexually assaulted (made to have sex by coercion or physical force) by the time they graduated. This number is higher than the one-in-five FBI statistic above.

As the old saying goes: "forewarned is forearmed." If you use common sense, learn the techniques in this book, don't drink or take drugs to the point of insensibility, and watch out for date rape drugs, your risk of rape becomes relatively safe.

Understanding Alcohol

So many high school and freshman people who drink beer think because they can remain moderately coherent after a few bottles that they have the capacity for liquor. It is this fallacy and misunderstanding about alcohol that often leads women to become so drunk, that they are incapable of giving consent to intercourse.

In my day in college, there were no date-rape drugs, but there was plenty of alcohol. Many college men offered dates drinks made from Bacardi 151 Rum. This was ultra-high proof alcohol (151 proof). Wikipedia states Bacardi 151 was finally discontinued in 2016 because so many lawsuits arose from the drink bursting into flames. If it got near a lighter, lit cigarette, candle, or other flame sources up it went. Imagine how many bottles of beer (4% to 6% alcohol by volume) it would take to equal one glass of 151 proof Bacardi!

In the U.S., alcohol is measured by proof or by "abv" (alcohol by volume). ABV is one half the proof. Thus, the traditional 86 proof whiskey is 43% alcohol by volume.

Historically, most alcoholic beverages in the early 20th century were drunk straight. You drank bourbon, scotch, gin and the like over ice. During Prohibition, when it was illegal to buy alcohol, a great many people bought "bootleg" liquor made illegally in local basements and small distilleries. They used to say the alcohol could peel the paint off a car, and in many cases, this "rock gut" whiskey would do just that.

To make the drink palatable people began mixing the alcohol with strong, sweeteners—hence the name "mixed drinks." With fruit juice, coke, or other non-alcoholic ingredients, you could hardly taste the ethanol alcohol. That is still true today.

Mix alcohol with fruit juice, coke or other such ingredients, and you will barely know how much alcohol you are drinking. Moreover, of course, the more you drink, the less you realize how much you are consuming.

Amount of Alcohol Per Drink

Alcohol is alcohol. The "standard" size of a glass of beer is 12 ounces, a glass of wine is five ounces, and a shot of hard liquor is 1.5 ounces. Each contains an equal amount of alcohol. Of course, since beer has less alcohol by volume, it takes 12 ounces of beer to equal the alcohol in a single of hard liquor.

A standard bottle of liquor (so-called Fifth or a 750ml bottle) contains 25.4 ounces. Since the standard bar shot is 1.5 ounces, if you went into a bar, it would take 17 drinks (shots) to finish the bottle.

When I was in a college fraternity, we poured 6 ounces per drink (the equivalent of 4 drinks). So, if you had two drinks at our fraternity it was the same as eight drinks of gin, vodka or whiskey. To put it in perspective, that would be the same as 1$\frac{1}{3}$ six-packs of beer. I know it was so in my fraternity, years ago and doubt it has changed. Further, more than a few "brothers" added four or five ounces of vodka to their date's beer. You have to be especially careful at college parties.

Many fraternities and college parties use large plastic beer cups to serve all their drinks. If you are handed four shots of vodka or rum with a mix of sweet fruit juice, like orange juice and pineapple, you probably won't taste the alcohol.

The average freshman woman is 18.4 years old, 125 pounds, and five foot four inches tall. According to the National Highway Traffic Safety Administration, if she drank just that one drink above within a half hour, her blood alcohol would be a .17, double the legal limit of drunk driving. The young freeshman would probably have trouble seeing clearly, might stumble often, and be hindered by a slow reaction time. If the drink hit her hard, the girl could also have confusion and dizziness.

The is no problem that you are drunk, as long as you know and expect to get drunk based on the amount of alcohol you consumed. The concern is when you are trying to stay relatively sober, you suddenly and often unexpectedly find yourself almost to the limit of being unable to give legal consent. This inebriation is the danger! You are in the "red zone" and are not capable of adequately protecting yourself from yourself.

Of course, everything said about alcohol is equally applicable to drugs. You never know what you are smoking, eating, digesting, or sniffing. It is even *possible* that your date might be the supplier of the drugs from a source he may not know or trust.

Why Women Get Drunk Faster than Men

A woman's body metabolizes liquor different than men. Most female college first-year students are less massive then men, and so just by lower weight volume, they get drunk faster than men. Additionally, pound-for-pound, women's bodies have a higher ratio of fat-to-water than men and so achieve a higher blood alcohol concentration than men. Finally, a 1990 study in the New England Journal of Medicine discovered that women produce just one-quarter of the amount of the hormone dehydrogenase as men. Dehydrogenase is used by the liver to break down alcohol, so only 25% of the volume of liquor is rendered harmless as compared to that of a man.

Everclear, the Dangerous Alcohol

Everclear is one of the highest proof drinks sold in the United States. Most vodka and gin sold in the U.S. is 80 proof (40% alcohol by volume). However, Everclear is 190 proof (95% alcohol by volume), and according to its manufacturer, it is colorless, odorless, and a neutral taste. As stated above, women get drunk faster than men. If you work out the mathematics, it's easy to see why the drink Everclear is so devastating to young women.

When Everclear is mixed with fruit juice, as is apparently done in some fraternities, it can't be detected. When served in a large plastic cup, a young woman could be drinking up to five ounces of Everclear. One beer is the equivalent of one ounce of liquor, and as 190 proof Everclear is twice as strong an ordinary gin or vodka, that one, single glass could be as powerful as drinking ten beers. As one fraternity brother boasted on the internet, "we at the House call it dynamite, since one or two drinks will blow open any girls legs." While the statement is crude and rude, it is also revealing how dangerous it might be for girls unsuspectingly drinking Everclear. You are ambushed and maybe helpless.

The Brock Turner Case

The California criminal case of *People v. Turner* is famous, and every college woman should be familiar with this 2016 case. Brock Turner was a Stanford University student-athlete who met a woman at a party. Her name was protected in the lawsuit and given the fictitious name of "Emily Doe."

Emily went to a party, had too much to drink (her blood alcohol was 2.2). She passed out, was taken outside by Mr. Turner, deposited behind a large dumpster, and while unconscious, was raped. At the penalty phase of the criminal trial, Ms. Doe read a compelling and detailed letter describing how the rape and the aftermath affected her life. The message went viral on the Internet (over 11 million reads), focusing considerable detail on crime. If you are interested in the case, search Google for *Brock Turner*. It is difficult for many to imagine why someone would want to rape anybody, but especially an unconscious woman, but it seems almost anything can happen when you drink.

Christine Blasey Ford

Christine Blasey Ford' testified in the Senate on September 27, 2018, during the hearing to confirm Judge Brett Kavanaugh to the U.S. Supreme Court. Her testimony is a warning to others.

> "When I got to the small gathering, people were drinking beer in a small living room on the first floor of the house. I drank one beer that evening. Brett and Mark were visibly drunk.
>
> Early in the evening, I went up a narrow set of stairs leading from the living room to a second floor to use the bathroom. When I got to the top of the stairs, I was pushed from behind into a bedroom. I couldn't see who pushed me. Brett and Mark came into the bedroom and locked the door behind them.
> There was music already playing in the bedroom. It was turned up louder by either Brett or Mark once we were in the room. I was pushed onto the bed and Brett got on top of me. He began running his hands over my body and grinding his hips into me.
>
> I yelled, hoping someone downstairs might hear me, and tried to get away from him, but his weight was heavy. Brett groped me and tried to take off my clothes. He had a hard time because he was so drunk, and because I was wearing a one-piece bathing suit under my clothes.
>
> I believed he was going to rape me. I tried to yell for help. When I did, Brett put his hand over my mouth to stop me from screaming."

Christine then testified why she did not tell her parents or anyone else.

"Brett's assault on me drastically altered my life. For a very long time, I was too afraid and ashamed to tell anyone the details. I did not want to tell my parents that I, at age 15, was in a house without any parents present, drinking beer with boys. I tried to convince myself that because Brett did [tried but did] not rape me, I should be able to move on and just pretend that it had never happened."

Act as You Will as a Senior

The odds of being raped in the first six weeks are so high; however, the likelihood of sexual assault during your senior year is so much less. The United States President's report, entitled "You Are Not Alone," found *75% of all college rapes occurred during the freshman and sophomore year.* Only a small percentage occurred during the senior year. As a senior, you have more experience and react more maturely and responsibly to higher risk situations.

If you are at a party with other friends, watch out for each other and don't let a girl disappear without knowing who she is with and if she is sober enough to give consent. Also, make sure all your friends get home safely. If you are walking in unlit or seldom used locations on campus, try to walk with a friend. If you do go out alone, let your friends know where you are and when you should return.

If you are looking for more security by using your smartphone, see the section entitled "Smartphone Applications" in the next chapter, Real Estate Agents. If such applications are warranted is a personal decision.

Conclusion

Re-read chapter 12, *Reduce the Risks in Your Life,* and concentrate carefully the sections about **"Saying 'No' Correctly,"** **"Date Rape**

Drugs," and "**Do Not Look Like a Victim**."

Also re-read chapter 30, Obnoxious Hook-Up in Car, and pay particular attention to the section on "Author's Advice" about the "**tipping point" when a date turns bad.** Finally, re-read chapter 20, **"If You Are Being Followed"** and chapter 13, **"Stay Safe in Nightclubs and Hookups."**

Being an adult, which is what you are at college, means great freedom. It also earns you the responsibility to take care of yourself. You no longer have parents watching and protecting you. During your freshman and sophomore year, you can enjoy a great deal of fun, and have sex *if* and *when* YOU want. Try to take the same steps and precautions that you will likely take as a senior.

CHAPTER 43

Real Estate Agents

Being a real estate broker or salesperson can be lucrative, but many insurance companies also classify it as a high-risk business. It is an occupation where you can meet a stranger, and an hour later you can be diving him about town to often empty buildings and homes where it could be just the two of you. Remember that in this high-risk profession, national statistics say one out of every five-to-six women has been or will be attacked during her lifetime. Add to that fact that you are in a higher than average risk, and you can see the need to exercise above ordinary caution.

You choose to be a sales agent or broker, but if you are seriously attacked and injured, I question whether you would feel safe enough to continue in that profession. In my opinion, you are risking your professional career and personal health (and in some cases your life) by feeling invulnerable and failing to take reasonable precautions. Of course, you can never be assured of being 100% safe in any occupation, but you can reduce the risks to acceptable levels without much inconvenience.

When I first started as a real estate broker (before I went to law school), I was *young*, *dumb*, and *hungry*. According to Burton Smith, then the State of California Real Estate Commissioner, I was one of the five youngest real estate brokers in the state of California. The *San Jose Mercury News*, the newspaper for Silicon Valley and the surrounding area, had chosen me as the *Real Estate Personality of the Week*. I was a guest speaker for one of the seminars for the National Association of Real Estate Boards (now called the National Association of Realtors). I felt invulnerable and took personal risks I wouldn't even consider now. I would meet strangers who wanted to see a house at night in vacant homes without any thoughts about my safety.

Worse, I was hungry, so I would accept clients that I should have known were statistically less likely to qualify to buy a home. However, at the time I thought clients meant sales, not realizing that mere quantity only resulted in wasting my time.

You owe it to yourself, your family and friends, and your profession, to take reasonable steps to lower your risk of being attacked. It doesn't take much to trouble to practice pro-actively. Three situations suggest special care: the first meeting of clients, secondly, showing home, and third, holding open houses.

Meet Clients at Your Office

Why Meet the Client

> The most significant safeguard you can do is to meet a new potential client at your office. Indeed some clients have a thousand excuses why they can't reach you at your office. They may say: "I am near to the house I want to see, so it makes no sense to come to your office." Alternatively, a potential client might say, "I'm too busy and in too short a period to travel to your office." The excuses go on and on, but they are all designed to avoid meeting your first. Most clients may be safe, but you cannot know that in advance. Why take the risk.

Tell them it is the standard practice to meet first in your office so you can show them the information they need to know before they see the house. Explain it may only take 15 minutes. If all else fails, try being honest, and explain in today's environment, you are in a high-risk business, and your insurance company (or employer) requires you first meet at your office.

If the client won't meet at your office, and demands meeting at the house, you will have no client control and probably will not be able to conclude a sale. More importantly, it is a "red flag" suggesting this may be a high-risk meeting. Finally, why would you want to take time showing a potential client property without at least qualifying him or her and finding out if they might be eligible for a loan? If they do not qualify, why waste your time. Your time is too precious to waste.

Meeting at the Office

When the client comes to the office, you would be wise to do two things. First, you should get a copy of his driver's license or another satisfactory picture ID. I found the easiest way is to have a simple "prospective buyer" sheet, that has six or seven simple questions like, name, address, phone, car license, and contacts.

The form should state it needs to be accompanied by a copy of their driver's license. I found that if the sheet has a picture of a driver's license and wording underneath that says "copy of license here," the client is more willing to allow his license to be copied. This Xerox is not a guaranty that the license is valid, and the person is a real prospect but is about as good as you can get.

If the person refuses, it is your first indication of a red flag that you cannot afford to ignore. If and when you leave your office with that new prospect, that form and copy of his license should be on top of your desk so others can see it and your client knows it is there.

Secondly, it would help if you would introduce the client to at least one other co-worker. Criminals do not like to be identified, and the more people who know them, the less likely they are the risk an illegal act. Most criminals know they will eventually get caught if they keep up their activities, so like everyone else, they seek to reduce the risk. There are too many easy targets to consider fixating on a high-risk "mark."

Showing Homes

Walk Behind the Client

When I was selling homes, it was traditional to go ahead of the client and show them the house. I always wanted to go first into a room, unless it was a small bedroom or space where I didn't want to emphasize how small the room was with several people inside.

As a ju-jitsu instructor, you don't want to have clients behind you when you have no idea what they are doing. Instead, let them lead the way and stay a few steps behind. You have far greater protection watching them.

Avoid Isolated Locations

You should be reluctant to go into a basement or outside shed with a new male client when the place is vacant. Let them go alone into those places. If a crime is going to occur, many times it is the most isolated places in a house.

In all fairness, you could be mugged or robbed as easily by a woman. However, statistics show such is not much risk.

Escape Route

It would be best if you always had your cell phone and keys with you at all times. (Smartphone applications are discussed later in this chapter.) Then, if you have to leave, you can do so immediately with everything you need. If you feel uncomfortable, trust your instincts. Tell the clients you have something in the car you want to show them; go out to your car and instead quietly drive away. Call the police or one of your male co-workers to close up the house.

You should also have a code word you can use to suggest to the office that you are in immediate danger. You can pick something as innocuous as, "I won't be able to make tomorrow's tour of the high-rise," or whatever is a good phrase for you. Your co-worker should then call the police, and maybe, if it is a good friend, come to the house to help you escape.

Possible Backup

Ideally, if you are showing a new client various new, vacant locations you would have a co-worker with you. The old saying of "safety in numbers" is true. However, as a practical matter, I know that co-workers are busy on their prospects and will seldom have the time and inclination to accompany you on a venture where there is little financial payoff for them. If you have an uncomfortable feeling and still feel the need to go, it might be wise to make it financially attractive to another agent (by offering them a percentage of the sale if it ever goes through). Statistics show that having someone accompany you is especially important at night.

Driving to the Location

Driving in one car is another one of those situations where you have to balance client control (having them in your car where you can continue selling them) versus safety (where they follow behind you in their car). You will have to evaluate that risk on a case-by-case basis.

Additionally, it would also be a good idea to have a "car locater" installed in your car. Many cars today come with that feature optional. It allows others to track your car's location.

Needless to say, you should park in front of the house where others can see your car, rather than in a driveway or side location that might not be fully visible from the street.

Empty Homes

If you are showing an utterly vacant house that has been unoccupied for some time, police recommend before entering that you look for any mail, cut telephone lines to the house, broken windows where someone could have entered, or broken doors. In specific locations and some parts of the country, one sometimes find squatters in the house. Indeed, if you expect a squatter, don't go in the house.

If you do unexpectedly encounter someone in the house, apologize saying you thought the house was unoccupied, and leave quickly. Do not ask questions or initiate a confrontation. It is not your responsibility to remove squatters. Remember, your goal is to reduce risks to your safety.

Leave and contact the owner or the police and let them deal with the squatter. They will evaluate if the squatter is there legally. Also, suggest the owner change the locks on the doors. Remember, you are not being paid enough to make their problem your problem.

Holding Open Houses

The Risk

Statistically speaking, the most significant risk in holding an open house is not injury to you, but theft. You can only be one place at a time, and thieves know that.

The ideal situation is to have two people at every open house. Stealing something is surprisingly easy when nobody is watching you. The second person need not even be a real estate broker or salesperson. It can be a teenager, a parent, a spouse, or a friend. It is just another pair of eyes, and most importantly, notice to others that you are not alone in the house.

Before open houses, you may wish to suggest to the home-owner that he or she removes all valuables and stores than at a neighbor's house for the day. While it might be embarrassing to discuss such a strategy, it is far better than having something taken, dealing with the insurance company, and facing an angry owner. In my day, each real estate office established their own rules regarding such situations.

Guard Your Purse

The day I started working, our office was abuzz with news of the saleswoman a week before who had her wallet stolen during an open house. Two women entered, and one walked in front of the agent asking a question. The other was just a mere three feet behind the agent, riffling through her purse, stealing her wallet. You might consider keeping your purse in the trunk of your car and having just your keys and cell phone with you at all times. Your goal is reducing your risk and making your life easier and safer.

Notify Neighbors

You would probably want to notify the neighbors that you are holding an open house. You are always trying to introduce yourself to potential new clients.

However, from a safety point of view, it is advisable to let neighbors know you will be next door. Benjamin Franklin wrote nearly two hundred and fifty years ago that the way to make someone who is not your friend like you is to ask them to do you a favor. It is still good advice. Ask the neighbors to keep an eye out for you.

Promotional Materials

Don't Advertise Sex

I know our real estate board at one time (and maybe they still do) recommend that women not look like they are advertising sex. By that, they mean, don't wear low cut blouses, flaunt your beauty in suggestive poses, and come on to potential men clients when together.

Our Board had a great sign to drive home the point: "asking what are you selling, homes or sex." In other words, don't give men a picture to fantasize being alone with you. Sadly, it may be only looking for trouble.

On a final note, I remember one husband and wife buyer I represented. The wife had changed agents because she felt the former woman broker was way to open and aggressive with her husband. It doesn't matter what the facts were; this was how the wife felt and why the former agent missed a sale.

Keep Personal Information off Your Flier:

Don't put your home address or other personal information on your fliers and business cards. Telephone numbers, such as your office number and cell phone number are acceptable but only list your office address. There may be just a few disturbed individuals running around, but all it takes is one to decide to visit you at home.

Smartphone Applications

Smartphone applications can make a woman safer, by giving her resources she doesn't now have, allowing her position to be traced, and alerting others if you don't respond when they expect you. The applications ("apps") are changing all the time, adding new features, and making them easier to use. Some apps will work on any smartphone; others will only work on certain operating systems or with specific phone manufacturers. Some cost and others are free, but a woman would be wise to investigate and determine if they are appropriate.

Some apps will use the smart phone's location services to tell others where you are at all times. They can even send a real-time map of where you are. Others can be programmed to notify designated friends or family (or even the police) if you do not respond by a particular time. The premises is that if you were safe, you would have responded to your phone app. Other programs can simulate a call to you so you can use the dummy phone call all as an excuse to leave.

Some phones are sophisticated enough to tell if you are running and will assume if you are doing so, you are in trouble and notify others. Other apps can tell your designated friend or family that you had arrived home safely at or by the time you specified. Some apps will assume if you have not responded by a specific time or upon activation, they will automatically record everything that is happening around, send those pictures to others, and indicate you may be in trouble. Some apps have a security button that will sound a loud alarm.

At least one major app, and probably many more, have a feature where for a price, someone will "actively" watch you every minute of your walking trip home. So often family members may watch you, but they may do so while doing the dishes or passively watching you. The paid app gives you professional watchers who actively view you during your trip. Your smartphone shows them your path and your steps as you walk and they actively monitor you.

Since you are relying so heavily on a cell phone, it would be wise to consider carrying an extra battery, or a battery enhancer that allows a battery to work extra hours. There is nothing worse than needing a cell phone in an emergency and finding you have a dead battery.

Conclusion

For broader and more comprehensive protection, re-read chapter 12, **Reduce the Risks in Your Life**, and concentrate carefully the sections about "**Saying 'No' Correctly**," "**Date Rape Drugs**," and "**Do Not Look Like a Victim**."

Also re-read chapter 30, **Obnoxious Hook-Up in Car**, and pay particular attention to the section on "Author's Advice" about the "**tipping point" when a date turns bad.** Finally, re-read chapter 20, **"If You Are Being Followed."**

Chapter 44

Nurses

Most nurses would agree that hospitals have a higher-than-average risk of rape and assault. You have patients that can be unpredictable and sometimes suffer from mental diseases or impairments. You have strangers who know nurses often leave shifts in the dark of night and walk to their cars. You have the risk of visitors and others hanging around the hospital, some high on drugs or angry at society. Hospitals tend to be notoriously understaffed. The list goes on, all of which makes your job high-risk. According to the U.S. Bureau of Labor Statistics, almost half of all violent attacks at the workplace are against nurses.

For simplicity, you have three major risks. The first is a garden variety attack by a hospital "visitor" looking to rob or rape you. The second is an attack by a patient, often by one who is permanently or temporarily mentally impaired. The third, often buried from consideration, is the risk to your job if you defend yourself from a patient attack in any way other than the "hospital recommended procedure."

Third-Person Attacks

This whole book is about attacks by others, and the best thing you can do is learn and study the self-defense techniques in the other chapters. I suggest learning one technique a week, so you are not overwhelmed. When you go out to your car a night, walk down deserted hallways, or travel through isolated locations with poor light, you would be wise to be on high alert. Don't just walk blindly along with your head down, fumbling in your purse or reading a book or patient chart, oblivious to your surroundings.

If you have to walk to your car a night, you should ask the hospital to assign someone escort you. It is just not worth the risk, and it only takes a few minutes for the hospital to obtain a guide for you.

If you want more security from your smartphone, see the section in the previous chapter about Real Estate Agents. It discusses the various types of cell phones applications ("apps") and the special protections these apps offer.

Attacks by Patients

Nurses, in general, have a much higher than average risk of attack. However, specific nursing positions have an incredibly high number of attacks. Some hospitals teach a unique course on handling difficult patients, but many do not even offer that level of protection.

Unfortunately, in my experience of teaching nurses, such courses appear designed to protect the patient more than the nurse. In my opinion: hospitals care more about lawsuits by patients, feel it is the nurse's job to protect patients, believe aggression can be de-escalated by talking, and assume nurses can defend themselves by "proper" nursing procedure.

There are some necessary safety precautions that you should always observe. Try to keep your back to an exit with the patient in front of you. You need a way to escape if the patient comes at you. If that is not possible, call in help from a co-worker. It is a question of how much risk are you willing to take for your job and how dangerous do you view the potential consequences if you are attacked. React wrong, and you put your job risk, and sometimes even the ability to enjoy the rest of life pain-free.

If you have a bad feeling about a patient, do not go in the room alone. Have another nurse stand by the door. The same rules in chapter 11 about *Reduce the Risks in Your Life* are equally applicable inside and outside of the hospital setting. Many nurses are injured because they thought they could handle the situation and patient and found out too late that their hubris resulted in significant injury.

I had a good friend, a psych nurse, who was overly busy one day and didn't want to wait to call for help. The patient grabbed her, and they both went down together. The rest of her life my friend had a terrible and painful back injury, which eventually required that she retire from nursing. The injury limited her life-activities and caused her pain almost every day.

The chapter *The Five Mandatory Rules* discusses how to stand with your strong point aimed at your opponent's weak point, the 90° angle to the line between his or her ankles. I recommend keeping that stance as much as possible to reduce your risk of being grabbed, falling, or struck by a patient.

Attacking a Patient in Self-Defense

This next section is to help you avoid being fired from your job. Attacking a patient, even in self-defense, generally leads to a sad result and a very challenging job situation. You need to understand what rights you have and how many remedies are denied to you.

The most obvious question is what self-defense is? It varies between states. In some states, if you have a choice of defending yourself and a reasonable means of escape, you are required to disengage and leave the scene. You can only protect yourself when you cannot reasonably get away. Other states follow the "stand your ground rules," which allows you to protect yourself without having to consider escape.

In most states, you can only use reasonable force to defend yourself. If you strike the person and he stops his attack, you are not allowed to keep beating on him. If you do so, you now become the aggressor and are liable for the excess attack. On the other hand, some states even allow you to use deadly force in your defense even if you are not attacked with life-threatening force. The law varies so widely you would need to check your state's statutes or with a local attorney.

Not uncommonly, a nurse wants to know if she can strike or otherwise attack a patient in defending yourself. Indeed, in the street, if you are attacked, you have the right to protect yourself with reasonable force. However, in a hospital setting, the law holds that your rights, especially with mentally ill patients, are not so clear-cut. I would recommend when you first start your job, that you ask the hospital's legal department for their answer.

First of all, most hospitals have prescribed rules that prohibit striking a patient. As one nurse said to me, "the hospital expects me to allow, the patient to beat on me, and to take it since I can't injure the patient. Hell, sometimes I feel like a punching bag hanging from the ceiling just waiting to be struck."

If you do injure the patient, regardless of circumstances, the hospital might assume you violated their rules and protocol that requires you to de-escalate the situation with proper conversations. In my opinion, the hospital's standard position seems to be that if you hit a patient, you are liable. The issue is not what is fair and reasonable, but what situation you might face if you do strike a patient.

The Federal Regulations

Let's get practical for a minute. It is sometimes hard to convince nurses how little power they have in striking a patient, even in self-defense. If you understand the hospital's restrictions, it may make it easier to comprehend why the hospital seems so unsympathetic to a nurse forced to defend herself.

Possibly the closest regulations you are going to find on the subject comes from the Centers for Medicare & Medicaid Services. Almost all hospitals, nursing homes, and other senior healthcare centers admit Medicare and Medicaid patients and are therefore bound by these federal regulations.

You can Google the Internet or look in most law libraries for the Code of Federal Regulations ("CFR"). It's an extensive set of books, and you want the volume containing title 42. In short, a Medicare or Medicaid patient has individual rights, and if those rights are violated, the hospital can be fined or otherwise punished. In my opinion, there is an exception when the hospital can prove: (1) it established hospital policies in accord with federal code, and (2) you, the nurse, on your own, violated those policies. In other words, the hospital might try to claim it is all your fault. It gives you some idea of the power you are challenging. Below represents some of the Medicare and Medicaid codes.

> "All patients have the right to be free from physical or mental abuse, and corporal punishment. All patients have the right to be free from restraint or seclusion, of any form, imposed as a means of coercion, discipline, convenience, or retaliation by staff. Restraint or seclusion may only be imposed to ensure the immediate physical safety of the patient, a staff member, or others and must be discontinued at the earliest possible time." 42 CFR §482.13(e).

A restraint is in part defined as: "Any manual method, physical or mechanical device, material, or equipment that immobilizes or reduces the ability of a patient to move his or her arms, legs, body, or head freely" 42 CFR §482.13(e)(1)(i)(A). The "restraint or seclusion may only be used when less restrictive interventions have been determined to be ineffective to protect the patient a staff member or others from harm." 42 CFR §482.13(e)(2). "The type or technique of restraint or seclusion used must be the least restrictive intervention that will be effective to protect the patient, a staff member, or others from harm." 42 CFR §482.13(e)(3).

Additionally, if all the above is not enough, the code of federal regulations goes on the state that:

"The use of restraint or seclusion must be (i) In accordance with a written modification to the patient's plan of care; and (ii) Implemented in accordance with safe and appropriate restraint and seclusion techniques as determined by hospital policy in accordance with State law. 42 CFR §482.13(e)(4).

The code continues by requiring the "use of restraint or seclusion must be in accordance with the order of a physician or other licensed independent practitioner who is responsible for the care of the patient ... and authorized to order restraint or seclusion by hospital policy in accordance with State law." 42 CFR §482.13(e)(5).

The reason why you must document and state why restraint was necessary, besides the requirements above, is that the code says:

"The attending physician must be consulted as soon as possible if the attending physician did not order the restraint or seclusion." 42 CFR §482.13(e)(7).

"When restraint or seclusion is used for the management of violent or self-destructive behavior that jeopardizes the immediate physical safety of the patient, a staff member, or others, the patient must be seen face-to-face within 1 hour after the initiation of the intervention" by a physician or qualified nurse to evaluate the patient and the situation. CFR §482.13(e)(12).

Loss of Job

Even so, can the hospital fire me for protecting myself? In most states, including California, absent an employment contract for a specific length of time, you are considered an "at will employee." At will means an employer, including a hospital, can fire you at *any time* for almost *any reason* (except for race, religion and other protected forms of discrimination). Strike a patient in self-defense, and the hospital will probably claim you violated their hospital's rules and may fire you on the spot. From your point of view, it may seem that fairness has nothing to do with the situation.

If you do strike or restrain a patient, many attorneys recommend two immediate strategies. First, thoroughly document the violence in the patient's chart. Then contact your supervisor to report the attack and self-defense, and then report the same to your hospital's security service. If you are seriously injured, many recommend calling the police. Finally, you should be examined by a doctor for medical injuries, even if you do not appear to be hurt. Be sure to note any mental anguish or trauma even if you are physically uninjured. Memorize the next sentence. *You are building the file to protect yourself.*

In one well known California court case, a nurse was injured by a patient, and that nurse sued the patient. John Muir is a large hospital in Walnut Creek, a town in the San Fransisco Bay Area. John Muir

Hospital requested the nurse drop the lawsuit, and when she refused the nurse was fired. The court upheld the firing. *Jersey v. John Muir Medical Center*, 97 Cal. App. 4th 814, 118 Cal. Rptr. 2d 807 (2002). The hospital sent the nurse the following letter:

> "It has recently been brought to our attention that you have elected to file a lawsuit against one of our patients whom you allege assaulted you. In investigating this matter I find that the patient in question was a head trauma patient on our Rehab Unit. As you are well aware, it is not uncommon for head trauma patients to exhibit erratic and sometimes violent behavior due to their medical condition, and as such they cannot be held responsible for their actions.
>
> The mission of this organization states that we are dedicated to improving the health of the communities we serve with quality and compassion. Suing a patient who cannot be held accountable for his actions because of a medical or psychological condition fits neither our mission nor its values. We expect you as a provider of patient care to assist our patients through their acute stages of illness and support them as they move through the health care continuum. Suing patients for non-intentional behavior does not meet these goals.
>
> We cannot allow you to remain in our employ at the same time you pursue this lawsuit against our patient, due to the conflict of interest. If we do not receive written confirmation from you within one week of the date of this letter that you have dropped your lawsuit against the patient, we will presume you have resigned your position."

In my opinion, most hospitals will probably respond as indicated above. As a nurse, be realistic about what your hospital or employer might do.

Conclusion

For broader and more comprehensive protection, re-read chapter 12, **Reduce the Risks in Your Lif**e, and concentrate carefully the sections about "**Saying 'No' Correctly**," "**Date Rape Drugs**," and "**Do Not Look Like a Victim**."

Also re-read chapter 30, **O**bnoxious Hook-Up in Car, and pay particular attention to the section on "Author's Advice" about the "**tipping point" when a date turns bad.** Finally, re-read chapter 20, **If You Are Being Followed,** and chapter 13, **Staying Safe in Nightclubs and Hookup**s."

Appendix

This   appendix is for those nurses who want more inforamtion on the risks they face, but otherwise is not essential reading. This entire book covers information on self-defense and the protection of women. However, nurses have, in my opinion, failed to understand and appreciate the risk they face in everyday work.

This appendix intends to help dispel the notion of safety. Nursing has a higher risk than other jobs, and it becomes your responsibility to protect yourself and conduct your nursing activities with an awareness of the heightened risk. You can't just blindly assume you will be safe, nor can you ignore common sense and necessary protective skills.

If you are injured or threatened on the job, you can burn out or leave the profession because of fear. You will then lose an occupation for which you were trained. Self-awareness and protective training can make all the difference in the world.

Cause of Increased Risk

Why is nursing such a dangerous occupation in relation to most other jobs in the US economy? National Institute of Occupational Safety and Health (NIOSH) has extensively studied the issue and issued six reasons:

1. The hospitals and the professional in general focus most on patient care and satisfaction, and such problems have a much greater concern than nurse safety.

2. The hospitals and other facilities present themselves as a self-regulating industry looking out for and created a safe environment for its workers. As such, the government and other safety institutions have not given nurses the protection and mandatory regulation that, perhaps, workers require.

3. There is a false belief in hospitals and nursing facilities that the work is safe, and attacks are rare and unpredictable occurrences that can't be stopped. Even though the nursing profession is mainly female-dominated, aggression from patients and patient families is far too high to ignore. Yet, the level of safety classes and skills do not meet the realities of the job. NOISH said one cause of workplace violence is "[s]taff shortages, increased patient morbidities, exposure to violent individuals, and the absence of strong workplace violence prevention programs and protective regulations are all barriers to eliminating violence against healthcare workers."

4. The hospitals focus on curative medicine as opposed to preventive treatment, and this culture seeps over into "occupational health and safety."

5. In general, there is a low rate of unionization in the health industry and a lower rate of control over the nurse's patient volume, overtime, stress, and other job duties and safety.

6. Finally, the hospital administration, currently and historically, has been male-dominated, and the men have been slow and reluctant to understand the stress and risk to the nurses fully.

Dangerous Patients

Lastly, NOISH lists the types of patients who are most likely to engage in physical assaults on nurses. As NIOSH states, "It is important to realize that, although some psychiatric diagnoses are associated with violent behavior, most people who are violent are not mentally ill, and most people who are mentally ill are not violent. Substance abuse is a major contributor to violence in populations both with and without psychiatric diagnoses."

The list below of potentially dangerous actors is verbatim from the NOISH website:

- are under the influence of drugs or alcohol
- are in pain
- have a history of violence
- have cognitive impairment
- are in the forensic (criminal justice) system
- are angry about clinical relationships, e.g., in response to perceived authoritarian attitude or excessive force used by the health provider
- have certain psychiatric diagnoses and/or medical diagnoses.

Categories of Violence

The National Institute of Occupational Safety and Health (NIOSH) classifies violence against nurses into four categories. To me, violence is violence. However, the classification is essential if you want to do any research or investigation into the area of physical attacks on nurses. The four types are listed below, and verbatim, from the NIOSH website.

1. **Type 1: Criminal Intent.** In Type 1 violence, the perpetrator has no legitimate relationship to the business or its employees, and is usually committing a crime in conjunction with the violence (robbery, shoplifting, trespassing). For example: a nurse assaulted in the hospital parking garage, or a home health care nurse is mugged while conducting a home visit. In health care settings Type I violence occurs less frequently compared to other types of violence.

2. **Type 2: Customer/Client**. Type 2 violence is the most common in healthcare settings. This course considers the customer/client relationship to include patients, their family members, and visitors, and will be referred to as CLIENT-ON-WORKER VIOLENCE. Research shows that this type of violence occurs most frequently in emergency and psychiatric treatment settings, waiting rooms, and geriatric settings, but is by no means limited to these.

3. **Type 3: Worker-on-Worker**. Type 3 violence between coworkers is commonly referred to as lateral or horizontal violence. It includes bullying, and frequently manifests as verbal and emotional abuse that is unfair, offensive, vindictive, and/or humiliating though it can range all the way to homicide. Work-

er-on-worker violence is often directed at persons viewed as being "lower on the food chain" such as in a supervisor to supervisee or doctor to nurse though incidence of peer to peer violence is also common.

4. **Type 4: Personal Relationship**. In Type 4 violence, the perpetrator has a relationship to the nurse outside of work that spills over to the work environment. For example, the husband of a nurse follows her to work, orders her home and threatens her, with implications for not only this nurse but also for her coworkers and patients.

Conclusion

The NOISH website offers a well-reasoned summary. "To keep the therapeutic relationship intact, a nurse may need to set limits on behavior if inappropriate behavior is exhibited. Many nurses ignore the inappropriate behavior, but in doing so, perpetuate it." In other words, when there is a threat of violence or violence, you can't ignore it, figuring it is too much trouble to report such acts. Lack of action is condoning and allowing such behavior. Further, you need to forcefully and explicitly point out to the patient or perpetrator that such activities are not tolerated.

If your facilities do not have documents to report such abhorrent activities, NIOSH offers the following forms that can be used or modified as appropriate.

Violence Incident Report Forms

Sample 1
The following items serve merely as an example of what might be used or modified by employers in these industries to help prevent workplace violence. (Sample/Draft—Adapt to your own location and business circumstances.)

Confidential Incident Report

To:_____ Date of Incident:_____

Location of Incident *(Map/sketch on reverse side or attached)*:_____

From:_____ Phone:_____ Time of Incident:_____

Nature of the Incident (*"X" all applicable boxes*):
❑ Assaults or Violent Acts:____Type "I"____Type "2"____Type "3"____Other
❑ Preventative or Warning Report
❑ Bomb or Terrorist Type Threat   ❑ Yes   ❑ No
❑ Transportation Accident   ❑ Contacts with Objects or Equipment
❑ Falls   ❑ Exposures   ❑ Fires or Explosions   ❑ Other
Legal Counsel Advised of Incident? ❑ Yes ❑ No   EAP Advised? ❑ Yes ❑ No
Warning or Preventative Measures? ❑ Yes ❑ No
Number of Persons Affected:_____

(For each person, complete a report; however, to the extent facts are duplicative, any person's report may incorporate another person's report.)
Name of Affected Person(s):_____Service Date:_____
Position:_____Member of Labor Organization? ❑ Yes ❑ No
Supervisor:_____Has Supervisor Been Notified? ❑ Yes ❑ No
Family:_____ Has Been Notified by:_____? ❑ Yes ❑ No
Lost Work Time? ❑ Yes ❑ No   Anticipated Return to Work:_____
Third parties or non-employee involvement *(include contractor and lease employees, visitors, vendors, customers)*? ❑ Yes ❑ No

Nature of the Incident
Briefly describe: (1) event(s); (2) witnesses with addresses and status included; (3) location details; (4) equipment/weapon details; (5) weather; (6) other records of the incident (e.g., police report, recordings, videos); (7) the ability to observe and reliability of witnesses; (8) were the parties possibly impaired because of illness, injury, drugs or alcohol? (were tests taken to verify same?); (9) parties notified internally (employee relations, medical, legal, operations, etc.) and externally (police, fire, ambulance, EAP, family, etc.).
Previous or Related Incidents of This Type? ❑ Yes ❑ No
Or by This Person? ❑ Yes ❑ No   Preventative Steps? ❑ Yes ❑ No
OSHA Log or Other OSHA Action Required? ❑ Yes ❑ No
Incident Response Team:_____
Team Leader:_____ _____
                        Signature   *Date*

Source: Reprinted with permission of Karen Smith Kalnbaum, Esq., Counsel to the Law Firm

Sample 2
The following items serve merely as an example of what might be used or modified by employers in these industries to help prevent workplace violence.

A reportable violent incident should be defined as any threatening remark or overt act of physical violence against a person(s) or property whether reported or observed.

1. Date:_____Day of Week:_____Time:_____ Assailant: ❑ Female ❑ Male

2. Specific Location:_____

3. Violence Directed Toward: ❑ Patient ❑ Staff ❑ Visitor ❑ Other
Assailant: ❑ Patient ❑ Staff ❑ Visitor ❑ Other
Assailant's Name:_____
Assailant: ❑ Unarmed ❑ Armed (weapon)

4. Predisposing Factors:
❑ Intoxication   ❑ Dissatisfied with Care/Waiting Time
❑ Grief Reaction   ❑ Prior History of Violence
❑ Gang Related   ❑ Other (Describe)_____

5. Description of Incident: ❑ Physical Abuse ❑ Verbal Abuse ❑ Other

6. Injuries: ❑ Yes ❑ No

7. Extent of Injuries:_____

8. Detailed Description of the Incident:_____

9. Did Any Person Leave the Area because of Incident?
❑ Yes ❑ No ❑ Unable to Determine

10. Present at Time of Incident:
❑ Police Name of Department:_____
❑ Hospital Security Officer

11. Needed to Call:
❑ Police Name of Department:_____
❑ Hospital Security

12. Termination of Incident:
Incident Diffused ❑ Yes ❑ No   Police Notified ❑ Yes ❑ No
Assailant Arrested ❑ Yes ❑ No

13. Disposition of Assailant:
❑ Stayed on Premises ❑ Escorted off Premises ❑ Left on Own ❑ Other

14. Restraints Used: ❑ Yes ❑ No Type:_____

15. Report Completed By:_____ Title:_____
Witnesses:_____
Supervisor Notified:_____ Time:_____

Please put additional comments, according to numbered section, on reverse side of form.

Source: Reprinted with permission of the Metropolitan Chicago Healthcare Council, *Guidelines for Dealing with Violence in Health Care*, Chicago, IL, 1995.

Appendix A

Use of Book for
Men's Self-Defense

After publication of the first edition, several people asked me if the book could be used for men. The book is obviously oriented towards women, and the text is especially geared to women, however, the ju-jitsu and karate techniques and equally applicable to men.

The only significant change for men would be special, detailed emphasis on punching, kicking and blocking (chapters 6-8). These arts are so necessary for men, yet warrant only mild concern for women. Mem would either need outside instruction on self-defense or a good book on Karate, such as *Dynamic Karate*, by N. Nakayama.

I told those people if I was teaching a course for men using this book, I would follow the program below:

I. Basic Escapes

1.	Escape from Headlock	Ch. 36
2.	Escape from Hammerlock	Ch. 37
3.	Escape from Full Nelson	Ch. 38
4.	Wrist Escapes	Ch. 2

II. Ju-Jitsu/Karate Principles

III. Advanced Escapes

About the Author

Ted H. Gordon started in ju-jitsu in 1957 in what was then the only San Francisco dojo (martial art's studio) that would teach non-Asian students. Ted earned a first-degree black belt in 1965 and his third-degree black belt in Ju-jitsu in 1971. Mr. Gordon also has a brown belt in Japanese Karate.

Educationally, Ted has a B.S., M.B.A., and J.D. degrees. He is the author of many books, including *California Real Estate Law: Text and Cases*, now in its 9th edition.

Ted is a guest instructor at Fight Ready in Scottsdale, Arizona.

Index

Index

Made in United States
Orlando, FL
05 September 2022

22028155R00161